The Story of Joseph: Genesis 37-50

Genesis, Volume 4

Dr Andrew C S Koh

Published by Dr. Andrew C S Koh, 2022.

Table of Contents

Dedicated to my wife, my sons, my daughters-in-law, my grandsons,
my granddaughters, and to the glory of God

Copyright

Scan QR code for a free book

"DR ANDREW C S KOH HAS DONE A WONDERFUL JOB OF BRINGING THE BIBLE TO LIFE IN HIS BOOKS" ROWAN S CALICH
GRATEFUL TO BE LISTED IN THE MALAYSIA BOOK OF RECORDS
for having the
MALAYSIA BOOK OF RECORDS
MOST BOOKS PUBLISHED AND RELEASED ON AMAZON IN A YEAR (2021)
DR ANDREW C S KOH

Preface

Genesis contains a timeless story about Joseph, a tale that has been resonating throughout history. It is a story filled with dreams, destiny and trials, as well as a faith that transcends time and space. The Genesis 37-50 account of Joseph's story has been a source of inspiration and reflection for many years. This story aims to reflect the complexity of human life while also capturing Joseph's journey.

In telling this incredible story, my goal was not to simply recreate history but to emphasize Joseph's timeless messages. Joseph is more than his colorful coats or grand palaces. He represents universal struggles like forgiveness, perseverance and faith in a divine plan. In these pages, Joseph's humanity, his doubts, and his unwavering faith are explored with vivid imagery and nuanced characters development. I wanted to make the characters and setting of this ancient tale vivid and tangible.

Through this retelling of Joseph's story, I hope to inspire you as you reflect on his struggles and choices while gaining timeless wisdom. These pages will provide you with new perspectives and a deeper understanding of Joseph's journey, no matter what your background is. The story of Joseph reminds us to live our lives with meaning, even when we are facing difficult situations. Joseph's story can provide us with guidance and insights to help guide our lives in a better direction.

Shalom and God bless you in your journey of faith.

Dr. Andrew C S Koh

Testimonials

I really enjoyed this daily devotional. I love the format, the educational content, and the concept. I also deeply enjoy the prayers within the daily studies. An excellent book!, Jennifer Surdam.

The Story of Joseph from Dr. Andrew C S Koh is a very good explanation of Joseph's life from Genesis 37 to 50. A nice book to get a little better understanding of the story of Joseph, Ellen Ebieze.

I like how Dr. Koh regularly examines the timeline to help us understand Joseph's role in the Bible's history. Joseph is a great example for Christians. Carol Howard.

A valuable tool for any Christian. Short and sweet, yet packed with all the essential details. Robert C Foland.

I appreciate Dr. Koh's periodic timeline review, which helps us understand Joseph's role in the overall history of the Bible. C Hoqard.

A great study guide and a great time to reflect on where my life is heading. I would recommend this book to anyone wanting a deeper understanding of Joseph, Kevin Booker.

This book is an invaluable resource for understanding the Bible scriptures, specifically the Life of Joseph. A very enlightening read, Rowan E Creech.

These Biblical truths are presented to the reader in an easy-to-understand devotion, allowing the reader to apply biblical truths to our contemporary living. PAR.

The author stayed as close to scripture as possible. I thoroughly enjoyed this life-like journey through Israel, Tiffany Townsend.

A great read about the story of Joseph. Well written and explained concerning the bible. There are beautiful prayers after each very meaningful chapter. I recommend this book to other readers, Sharmani Jeyaram,.

Introduction to Joseph

Hebrews for Genesis is Bereshit, which means beginning. Genesis is the book of beginnings, the beginning of the universe, the beginning of creation, the beginning of humans, the beginning of life, the beginning of sin, the beginning of death, etc. There are many firsts in Genesis, the first human being, the first marriage, the first sin, the first death, the first murder, etc. When you read the Book of Genesis, watch out for all the first. The Book of Genesis can be divided into 2 sections. Section 1, Genesis 1 to 11, primeval history, from Adam to Abraham, and section2, Genesis 12 to 50, patriarchal history, from Abraham to Joseph. This book only covers Genesis 37-50, the narrative of the life, adventures, and faith journey of Joseph.

Genre, author, recipients

The genre of Genesis is historical narrative and chronological genealogy. The author of Genesis was believed to be Moses, who also authored Exodus, Leviticus, Numbers, and Deuteronomy. These five books are collectively called the Pentateuch. The recipients were the Israelites of the wilderness wandering from Exodus to Deuteronomy

Outline of Genesis 37-50

Genesis 37: Joseph's dreams

Genesis 38: downward spiral, death, incest

Genesis 39: the LORD was with Joseph

Genesis 40: master of dreams

Genesis 41: from prisoner to prime minister

Genesis 42: from Canaan to Egypt

Genesis 43: the reunion of 12 brothers

Genesis 44: final test

Genesis 45: forgiveness and reconciliation

Genesis 46: family move

Genesis 47: Jacob's sojourn in Egypt

Genesis 48: adoption of Ephraim and Manasseh

Genesis 49: the death of Jacob

Genesis 50: the death of Joseph

Contents

Genesis 37
Dreamer

Genesis 37 begins a new section zeroing in on the life of Joseph. The baton of faith was passed down from Abraham, Isaac, Jacob, and Jacob's twelve sons or the Patriarchs. The most outstanding Patriarch was Jacob's eleventh son, Joseph. Genesis 37- 50 is the narrative on the life of Joseph. Genesis 49 ends with the death of Jacob, Genesis 49:33. Genesis 50 ends with the death of Joseph, Genesis 50:26.

Verses 1-4, 1 Jacob lived in the land of his father's travels, in the land of Canaan. 2 This is the history of the generations of Jacob. Joseph, being seventeen years old, was feeding the flock with his brothers. He was a boy with the sons of Bilhah and Zilpah his father's wives. Joseph brought an evil report of them to their father. 3 Now Israel loved Joseph more than all his children, because he was the son of his old age, and he made him a tunic of many colours. 4 His brothers saw that their father loved him more than all his brothers, and they hated him, and couldn't speak peaceably to him.

Reflection

After his return from Haran, Jacob lived in the promised land Canaan. By now, Jacob had 12 sons. Joseph was the eleventh and Benjamin was the twelfth and youngest son. The seventeen-year-old Joseph was feeding his father's flock with half-brothers in the field. He complained to his father that his half-brothers were behaving badly. Jacob or Israel loved Joseph and Benjamin more than the rest because they were his favourite wife, Rachel's sons. Jacob even made a multi-coloured tunic for Joseph to wear and his half-brothers were jealous. They hated Joseph and were not on talking (speaking) terms with him.

Verses 6-11, 5 Joseph dreamed a dream, and he told it to his brothers, and they hated him all the more. 6 He said to them, "Please hear this dream which I have dreamed: 7 for behold, we were binding sheaves in the field, and behold, my sheaf arose and also stood upright; and behold, your sheaves came around, and bowed down to my sheaf." 8 His brothers asked him, "Will you indeed reign over us? Will you indeed have dominion over us?" They hated him all the more for his dreams and for his words. 9 He dreamed yet another dream, and told it to his brothers, and said, "Behold, I have dreamed yet another dream: and behold, the sun and the moon and eleven stars bowed down to me." 10 He told it to his father and to his brothers. His father rebuked him, and said to him, "What is this dream that you have dreamed? Will I and your mother and your brothers indeed come to bow ourselves down to the earth before you?" 11 His brothers envied him, but his father kept this saying in mind.

Reflection

The LORD gave Joseph two dreams. In the first dream, he saw his brothers represented by eleven sheaves of wheat bowing down to him. In the second dream, he was his father, Jacob, mother, Leah, and brothers, represented by the sun, moon, and eleven stars, bowing down to him.

In Revelation 12:1, apostle John saw a vision of a woman clothed in the sun, standing on the moon under her feet, and wearing a crown of 12 stars. The woman represents the nation of Israel, the 12 stars represent the 12 patriarchs. Joseph's brothers hated him because of the dream. Even Jacob rebuked him for saying such a dream. Joseph's dreams were fulfilled when he became the prime minister of Egypt and they bowed down to him, Genesis 42:6.

Revelation 12:1, *"A great sign was seen in heaven: a woman clothed with the sun, and the moon under her feet, and on her head a crown of twelve stars."*

Genesis 42:6, *"Joseph was the governor over the land. It was he who sold to all the people of the land. Joseph's brothers came, and bowed themselves down to him with their faces to the earth."*

Verses 12-17, *12 His brothers went to feed their father's flock in Shechem. 13 Israel said to Joseph, "Aren't your brothers feeding the flock in Shechem? Come, and I will send you to them." He said to him, "Here I am." 14 He said to him, "Go now, see whether it is well with your brothers, and well with the flock; and bring me word again." So, he sent him out of the valley of Hebron, and he came to Shechem. 15 A certain man found him, and behold, he was wandering in the field. The man asked him, "What are you looking for?" 16 He said, "I am looking for my brothers. Tell me, please, where they are feeding the flock." 17 The man said, "They have left here, for I heard them say, 'Let's go to Dothan.'" Joseph went after his brothers and found them in Dothan*

Reflection

Israel was Jacob's new name. He told Joseph to look for his half-brothers who were feeding the flocks in Shechem. Joseph left Hebron and arrived at

Shechem. He did not find his brothers there. An unnamed man found Joseph wandering aimlessly and asked him whom he was looking for. Joseph replied that he was looking for his brothers and the man directed him to Dothan.

Joseph went to Dothan and found his brothers there. Dothan was located to the north of Shechem. Dothan in Hebrews means two wells and these two wells are still there today. This is the first time that Dothan is mentioned. Dothan is mentioned again in 2 Kings 6:13 in the narrative on Elisha.

2 Kings 6:13, *"Go and see where he is, that I may send and get him." He was told, "Behold, he is in Dothan."*

Verses 18-22, *18 They saw him afar off, and before he came near to them, they conspired against him to kill him. 19 They said to one another, "Behold, this dreamer comes. 20 Come now, therefore, and let's kill him, and cast him into one of the pits, and we will say, 'An evil animal has devoured him.' We will see what will become of his dreams." 21 Reuben heard it, and delivered him out of their hand, and said, "Let's not take his life." 22 Reuben said to them, "Shed no blood. Throw him into this pit that is in the wilderness but lay no hand on him"—that he might deliver him out of their hand, to restore him to his father.*

Reflection

As Joseph was approaching from a distance, his brothers conspired to murder him. They hated Joseph so much that they contemplated murdering him. They even thought of concealing their wicked act by saying that an animal had eaten Joseph. They thought this would put an end to Joseph's dreams. Reuben, the first born, came to Joseph's rescue. H managed to convince the rest not to kill Joseph but to throw him into a pit. He planned to come back later to rescue him on his own.

Verses 23-28, *23 When Joseph came to his brothers, they stripped Joseph of his tunic, the tunic of many colors that was on him; 24 and they took him, and threw him into the pit. The pit was empty. There was no water in it. 25 They sat down to eat bread, and they lifted up their eyes and looked, and saw a caravan of Ishmaelites was coming from Gilead, with their camels, bearing spices and balm and myrrh, going to carry it down to Egypt. 26 Judah said to his brothers, "What profit is it if we kill our brother and conceal his blood? 27 Come, and let's sell him to the Ishmaelites, and not let our hand be on him; for he is our brother, our flesh." His brothers listened to him. 28 Midianites, who were merchants, passed by, and they drew and lifted up Joseph out of the pit, and sold Joseph to the Ishmaelites for twenty pieces of silver. The merchants brought Joseph into Egypt.*

Reflection

When Joseph came to his brothers, they removed his multi-coloured tunic and threw him into an empty pit. Imagine how shocked Joseph must have been to be treated so brutally by his own brothers. When the brothers sat down to eat bread, a group of Ishmaelite traders came by with their caravans. Ishmaelites were descendants of Ishmael, the son of Abraham's concubine Hagar.

The Midianites were the descendants of Midian, son of Abraham's concubine Keturah. A group of Midianites traders also came along and took Joseph out of the pit. The brothers sold Joseph to the Ishmaelite traders for twenty pieces of silver. In today's language, this is called human traffickers!

Verses 29-33, 29 Reuben returned to the pit and saw that Joseph wasn't in the pit, and he tore his clothes. 30 He returned to his brothers, and said, "The child is no more; and I, where will I go?" 31 They took Joseph's tunic, and killed a male goat, and dipped the tunic in the blood. 32 They took the tunic of many colors, and they brought it to their father, and said, "We have found this. Examine it, now, and see if it is your son's tunic or not." 33 He recognized it, and said, "It is my son's tunic. An evil animal has devoured him. Joseph is without doubt torn in pieces.

Reflection

When Reuben who had left the scene came back and found that Joseph had been sold to the Ishmaelites, he was devastated. The brothers took Joseph's multi-coloured tunic and dripped it in goat's blood. They showed the blood-soaked tunic to Jacob and asked him to identify it. Jacob tore his clothes and believed that Joseph had died. They did not have DNA testing there and then. Jacob was reaping what he sowed. He deceived his father, Isaac. Now his own sons deceived him. What goes around, comes around.

Verses 34-36, "34 Jacob tore his clothes, and put sackcloth on his waist, and mourned for his son many days. 35 All his sons and all his daughters rose up to comfort him, but he refused to be comforted. He said, "For I will go down to Sheol to my son, mourning." His father wept for him. 36 The Midianites sold him into Egypt to Potiphar, an officer of Pharaoh's, the captain of the guard.

Reflection

Jacob mourned for his son Joseph and refused to be consoled. He tore his clothes, wore sackcloth, wept, and mourned for Joseph every day. Meanwhile, the slave traders took Joseph to Egypt and sold him to Potiphar, a high-ranking officer of Pharoah.

Jacob's family was a dysfunctional family, headed by a passive, weak, father, who played favouritism. He loved Joseph and Benjamin more than the rest. Sibling rivalry, strife, hatred, and jealousy were the order of the day.

Are you a father? Do you have a strong leadership? Do you practice favouritism among your children? Favouritism is a no-no.

Jacob reaped what he sowed. He deceived his father Isaac, and now his own sons came back to deceive him.

Joseph was a type of Christ. Jacob loved Joseph. God the Father loved Christ. Joseph's brothers hated him. The Jews hated Christ. The list goes on and on as we shall see as the narrative unfolds.

Application

Trust in God's plan even in tough times.

Joseph's story shows us to trust in the plan of God even in difficult situations and confusing circumstances. Though sold into slavery, Joseph eventually rose to become ruler in Egypt and saved many souls along his journey.

Think about times when things didn't go as you expected and how God might be using them for a bigger purpose.

Effective Strategies for Handling Jealousy and Favoritism

Jacob's favoritism towards Joseph and its effects on his brothers is evidence of their destructive potential.

Analyze your family relationships to ensure that everyone is being treated fairly. Alleviate any feelings of jealousy by cultivating contentment and gratitude for what you already possess.

The Power of Forgiveness

Joseph eventually let go of his anger towards his brothers, showing the value and benefits of forgiveness and reconciliation.

If you have people you need to forgive, think about how holding onto bitterness affects you. Take steps towards reconciliation and forgiveness.

Pride Can Harm

Joseph's initial arrogance about his dreams may have fueled their brothers' resentment of him.

Be humble about your successes and share them in ways that inspire and uphold others, rather than brag.

God's Sovereignty

No matter what people may do or think, God always works in accordance with His sovereign will and destinies. Even Joseph's brothers' intentions of harm were used by Him for His greater plans.

Remind yourself of God's sovereignty during difficult situations, trusting that He can turn any negative into positive.

Responding to Injustice

Joseph's response to his unjust treatment teaches us about integrity and resilience; he remained faithful to God despite his circumstances.

When faced with injustice or hardship, be sure to maintain your integrity and faith. Seek ways of strengthening yourself, so you can serve God regardless of difficult situations.

Thinking about these applications can help you understand your spiritual journey better and figure out how to handle life's challenges from a biblical point of view.

Prayer

Heavenly Father, thank You for giving us the opportunity to study the life of Joseph in the Book of Genesis. We pray for open eyes, open ears, open hearts, open minds, and open spirits to receive the revelation of Your Word. We pray for the anointing of the Holy Spirit who is our teacher, truth revealer, helper, and counsellor, in Jesus' name, Amen.

Genesis 38

Consequences of deception

Genesis 38 is a parenthesis, interlude, or excursus, from the Joseph narrative. After selling Joseph to the Ishmaelite/ Midianite human traffickers, Judah left his brothers and stayed with a man of Adullam. He went down the spiritual staircase and did things that should not be done.

The high drama of this chapter was death, incest, and spiritual decline. Judah's first and second son, Er, Onan, and his unnamed Canaanite wife died. Tamar deceived Judah to commit incest by disguising herself as a prostitute. The Joseph narrative resumed in Genesis 39.

Verses 1-5, 1 At that time, Judah left his brothers and went down to stay with a man of Adullam named Hirah. 2 There Judah met the daughter of a Canaanite man named Shua. He married her and made love to her; 3 she became pregnant and gave birth to a son, who was named Er. 4 She conceived again and gave birth to a son and named him Onan. 5 She gave birth to still another son and named him Shelah. It was at Cherib that she gave birth to him.

Reflection

For some unknown reasons, Judah left his brothers and went down to Canaan to live with Hirah, an Adullamite. Adullam was a Canaanite city. Hirah in Hebrews means a noble family.

Going to Canaan is going down into a spiritual decline. He befriended a Canaanite man and married a Canaanite woman, the daughter of Shua. Canaanites were not the covenant people of the LORD. The LORD forbade the Israelites to associate or intermarry with Canaanites.

Judah disobeyed the LORD. Shua conceived and bored Judah with three sons, Er, Onan, and Shelah. Shua in Hebrews means a cry for help. Er in Hebrews means watcher. Onan in Hebrews means force. Shelah in Hebrews means petition.

Verses 6-10, 6 Judah got a wife for Er, his firstborn, and her name was Tamar. 7 But Er, Judah's firstborn, was wicked in the Lord's sight; so the Lord put him to death.8 Then Judah said to Onan, "Sleep with your brother's wife and fulfill your duty to her as a brother-in-law to raise up offspring for your brother." 9 But Onan knew that the child would not be his; so whenever he slept with his brother's wife, he spilled his semen on the ground to keep from providing offspring for his brother. 10 What he did was wicked in the Lord's sight; so, the Lord put him to death also.

Reflection

Judah allowed his eldest son Er to marry Tamar. Tamar in Hebrews means date palm. Er was wicked in the LORD's sight and the LORD killed him. In that culture and age, when the first born died without a son, the next of kin must marry the widow and raise a son for the deceased.

This would ensure the continuity of the deceased family line for inheritance purposes. This is called the kinsman-redeemer. Judah ordered Onan to be Tamar's kinsman-redeemer, but Onan refused to play the role of a kinsman redeemer. It was wicked in the sight of the LORD and so, the LORD killed Onan too.

The marriage of Onan to Judah was the first example of levirate marriage in the Bible. Levirate means marriage to a brother-in-law. In Biblical times, if a woman outlived her husband without any son, she would marry her brother-in-law. The first son of that marriage would legally belong to the dead husband, Deuteronomy 25:5-6.

Deuteronomy 25:5-6, *"If brothers dwell together, and one of them dies and has no son, the wife of the dead shall not be married outside to a stranger. Her husband's brother shall go in to her, and take her as his wife, and perform the duty of a husband's brother to her. It shall be that the firstborn whom she bears shall succeed in the name of his brother who is dead, that his name not be blotted out of Israel."*

Verse 11-14, *11 Judah then said to his daughter-in-law Tamar, "Live as a widow in your father's household until my son Shelah grows up." For he thought, "He may die too, just like his brothers." So Tamar went to live in her father's household. 12 After a long time Judah's wife, the daughter of Shua, died. When Judah had recovered from his grief, he went up to Timnah, to the men who were shearing his sheep, and his friend Hirah the Adullamite went with him. 13 When Tamar was told, "Your father-in-law is on his way to Timnah to shear his sheep," 14 she took off her widow's clothes, covered herself with a veil to disguise herself, and then sat down at the entrance to Enaim, which is on the road to Timnah. For she saw that, though Shelah had now grown up, she had not been given to him as his wife.*

Reflection

Judah told his daughter-in-law to return to her father's house as a widow until his third son Shelah had grown up. However, Judah was not sincere and had no intention of giving Shelah to Tamar in marriage. He was afraid that Shelah too would die if he married Tamar.

As time went by, Judah's wife, the daughter of Shua passed away. After the grieving period was over, Judah went to Timnah with his friend Hirah. When Tamar heard that Judah was on his way to Timnah, she changed into a prostitute's attire and sat by the roadside at Enaim, waiting for Judah to pass by. She saw that Shelah had grown up but Judah had not kept his part of the deal.

Verses 15-19, *15 When Judah saw her, he thought she was a prostitute, for she had covered her face. 16 Not realizing that she was his daughter-in-law, he went over to her by the roadside and said, "Come now, let me sleep with you." "And what will you give me to sleep with you?" she asked. 17 "I'll send you a young goat from my flock," he said. "Will you give me something as a pledge until you send it?" she asked. 18 He said, "What pledge should I give you?" "Your seal and its cord, and the staff in your hand," she answered. So, he gave them to her and slept with her, and she became pregnant by him. 19 After she left, she took off her veil and put on her widow's clothes again.*

Reflection

Judah thought that Tamar was a prostitute because she had covered her face. Unknowingly, Judah demanded sex for payment from his own daughter-in-law, Tamer demanded payment and Judah agreed to pay her with a goat. Since she did not have a goat, Tamar demanded a security deposit. Judah agreed to give her his seal with its cord and his staff as security deposits until the goat was delivered. Tamar conceived through the incestuous union. She left the scene and put back on her widow's attire.

Verses 20-23, *20 Meanwhile Judah sent the young goat by his friend the Adullamite in order to get his pledge back from the woman, but he did not find her. 21 He asked the men who lived there, "Where is the shrine prostitute who was beside the road at Enaim?" "There hasn't been any shrine prostitute here," they said. 22 So he went back to Judah and said, "I didn't find her. Besides, the men who lived there said, 'There hasn't been any shrine prostitute here.'" 23 Then Judah said, "Let her keep what she has, or we will become a laughingstock. After all, I did send her this young goat, but you didn't find her."*

Reflection

Judah told his friend Hirah to go to Enaim and deliver the goat to the woman, but he was unable to trace her. The local people denied that there was any prostitute there. To prevent further embarrassment, Judah told Hirah to forget about the whole thing.

Verses 24-16, *24 About three months later Judah was told, "Your daughter-in-law Tamar is guilty of prostitution, and as a result, she is now pregnant." Judah said, "Bring her out and have her burned to death!" 25 As she was being brought out, she sent a message to her father-in-law. "I am pregnant by the man who owns these," she said. And she added, "See if you recognize whose seal and cord and staff these are." 26 Judah recognized them and said, "She is more righteous than I since I wouldn't give her to my son Shelah." And he did not sleep with her again.*

Reflection

Three months later Judah came to know that Tamar was pregnant. In anger, Judah demanded that Tamar be burnt to death for her sin. When Tamar appeared before Judah, she took out the seal, the cord, and the staff to prove that she was made pregnant by Judah himself. Judah was caught red-handed. He exclaimed that Tamar was more righteous than him. He admitted that he had not kept his promise to give Shelah to Tamar in marriage even though Shelah had grown up.

Verses 27-30, *27 When the time came for her to give birth, there were twin boys in her womb. 28 As she was giving birth, one of them put out his hand; so, the midwife took a scarlet thread and tied it on his wrist and said, "This one came out first." 29 But when he drew back his hand, his brother came out, and she said, "So this is how you have broken out!" And he was named Perez.30 Then his brother, who had the scarlet thread on his wrist, came out. And he was named Zerah.*

Reflection

Tamar gave birth to twins, Perez and Zerah. When Zerah put out his hand momentarily, the midwife tied a scarlet thread onto his hand. Perez was delivered first followed by Zerah.

Judah left his brothers, associated with a Canaanite whom the LORD forbade. He was unequally yoked. Paul warned Christians not to be unequally yoked with non-Christians, whether in business, marriage, or any ventures, 2 Corinthians 6:14.

2 Corinthians 6:14, *"Don't be unequally yoked with unbelievers, for what fellowship have righteousness and iniquity? Or what fellowship has light with darkness?"*

Judah reaped what he sowed. Earlier, he deceived Jacob that Joseph was killed by a wild animal. Now, Tamar deceived him on the road to Enaim. What goes around comes around.

Judah was hypocritical when he self-righteously condemned Tamar for being pregnant. It is easy to see the speck in other people's eyes and not see the log in our own eyes, Matthew 7:5.

Matthew 7:5, *"You hypocrite! First remove the beam out of your own eye, and then you can see clearly to remove the speck out of your brother's eye."*

Judah, Tamar, and Perez made it into the genealogy of Jesus Christ. That God would use two sinful people to be included in Christ's genealogy demonstrates His grace. Judah's character was questionable and Tamar was not even a Jew, yet Jesus picked them to be included in His genealogy. God is a God of grace. God justifies and saves sinners by grace through faith in Christ.

Matthew 1:3, *"Judah became the father of Perez and Zerah by Tamar. Perez became the father of Hezron. Hezron became the father of Ram."*

Application

Genesis 38 tells the story of Judah and Tamar. It provides valuable lessons and applications that relate to Joseph's story. This chapter, seemingly out of place with its overall scheme, nevertheless provides essential teachings.

Take Responsibility for Action Taken

Judah initially failed to acknowledge his actions in regard to Tamar. When he eventually acknowledged them, it showcased the significance of accepting responsibility for our mistakes.

Reflect on areas of your life where you might need to take responsibility for your actions. Try to make amends and learn from past mistakes.

Consequences of Deception

Deception is an underlying theme in this chapter, as both Judah and Tamar took part in deceptive acts to their detriment. The story highlights its potential harmful repercussions.

Strive for honesty and openness in life. Deceit can often create more problems and complications.

Righteousness and Justice are Important

Tamar's unconventional and desperate actions were fueled by her longing for fairness and moral values within her family. This underscores the importance of upholding righteousness and justice regardless of circumstances.

Fight for what is just and fair even when it is difficult. Seek God's direction when making decisions that adhere to His principles of justice.

Understanding the Importance of Upholding Promises

Judah's failure to keep his promise to Tamar regarding Shelah illustrated the significance of keeping one's commitments.

Review your commitments and follow through with them, building a reputation of reliability and trustworthiness in the process.

God's Redemptive Plan

Even with their mistakes, biblical characters continue to demonstrate God's redemptive power through their lives. Tamar being included as Jesus's lineage (Matthew 1:1-3) shows Him in action bringing redemption out of bleak situations.

Trust that God can redeem any situation, no matter how dire. Observe ways in which He may be working in your life to bring good out of challenging events.

Understanding Cultural Contexts

This story is deeply rooted in the culture and legal practices of its time period, such as levirate marriage. Understanding these contexts helps us understand their motivations and actions of characters within them.

As you read biblical narratives, take time to gain an understanding of their historical and cultural settings. This can provide additional insight into both their textual message and how it applies today.

In Genesis 38, you can find valuable lessons for living ethically, seeking justice, and trusting in God's power to redeem.

Prayer

Heavenly Father, thank You for Your presence, anointing, revelation, rebuke, teaching, correction, and training in righteousness. Thank You for Your mercy and grace. Thank You that Christ died for us when we were still sinners. Thank You for salvation, justification, the forgiveness of sins, and the promise of eternal life, in Jesus' name, Amen.

Genesis 39

Integrity in the face of temptation

The narrative of Joseph continued from Genesis 37 after the parenthesis of Genesis 38. Joseph was taken to Egypt by the Ishmaelites/ Midianites human traffickers and sold on the slave market.

Verses 1-5, *1 Joseph was brought down to Egypt. Potiphar, an officer of Pharaoh's, the captain of the guard, an Egyptian, bought him from the hand of the Ishmaelites that had brought him down there. 2 Yahweh was with Joseph, and he was a prosperous man. He was in the house of his master the Egyptian. 3 His master saw that Yahweh was with him and that Yahweh made all that he did prosper in his hand. 4 Joseph found favor in his sight. He ministered to him, and Potiphar made him overseer over his house, and all that he had he put into his hand.*

Reflection

Potiphar, an Egyptian officer of Pharoah bought Joseph from the slave traderss. The LORD was with Joseph and prospered him. Joseph handled the affairs of his master efficiently. Potiphar saw that Joseph was a Godly man and trusted him unreservedly. Potiphar liked Joseph and made him in charge of everything in his household.

Verses 5-7, *5 From the time that he made him overseer in his house, and over all that he had, Yahweh blessed the Egyptian's house for Joseph's sake. Yahweh's blessing was on all that he had, in the house and in the field. 6 He left all that he had in Joseph's hand. He didn't concern himself with anything, except for the food which he ate. Joseph was well-built and handsome. 7 After these things, his master's wife set her eyes on Joseph; and she said, "Lie with me."*

Reflection

God's blessing on Joseph overflowed to Potiphar until he was very prosperous. With Joseph running the affairs of his household, Potiphar did not have to do anything at all. Joseph's charm and good looks caught the attention of Mrs. Potiphar who tempted him day in and day out.

Verses 4-10, *8 But he refused, and said to his master's wife, "Behold, my master doesn't know what is with me in the house, and he has put all that he has into my hand. 9 No one is greater in this house than I am, and he has not kept back anything from me but you, because you are his wife. How then can I do this great wickedness, and sin against God?" 10 As she spoke to Joseph, day by day, he didn't listen to her, to lie by her, or to be with her.*

Reflection

Joseph was a Godly man. He overcame the temptation to sin and rejected her advances. He did not sin against God and did not betray the trust of Potiphar. Meanwhile Mrs. Potiphar kept on pestering Joseph to have sex with her.

Verses 11-18, *11 About this time, he went into the house to do his work, and there were none of the men of the house inside. 12 She caught him by his garment, saying, "Lie with me!" He left his garment in her hand and ran outside. 13 When she saw that he had left his garment in her hand, and had run outside, 14 she called to the men of her house, and spoke to them, saying, "Behold, he has brought a Hebrew in to us to mock us. He came in to me to lie with me, and I cried with a loud voice. 15 When he heard that I lifted up my voice and cried, he left his garment by me and ran outside." 16 She laid up his garment by her until his master came home. 17 She spoke to him according to these words, saying, "The Hebrew servant, whom you have brought to us, came in to me to mock me, 18 and as I lifted up my voice and cried, he left his garment by me, and ran outside."*

Reflection

One day when there was no one in the house, Mrs. Potiphar grabbed Joseph by his coat and forced him to have sex with her. Joseph ran out of the house leaving his coat in Mrs. Potiphar's hand. The woman summoned everyone back into the house and falsely alleged that Joseph had outraged her modesty using his coat as evidence.

In those days, there was no CCTV recording. Joseph was only a slave. He was in no position to defend himself in the court of law. There was no eyewitness to testify. Joseph had no way to clear his name. Only the LORD could vindicate him.

Verses 19-23, *19 When his master heard the words of his wife, which she spoke to him, saying, "This is what your servant did to me," his wrath was kindled. 20 Joseph's master took him and put him into the prison, the place where the king's prisoners were bound, and he was there in custody. 21 But Yahweh was with Joseph, and showed kindness to him, and gave him favor in the sight of the keeper of the prison. 22 The keeper of the prison committed to Joseph's hand all the prisoners who were in the prison. Whatever they did there, he was responsible for it. 23 The keeper of the prison didn't look after anything that was under his hand, because Yahweh was with him; and that which he did, Yahweh made it prosper.*

Reflection

When Potiphar heard Mrs. Potiphar's version of the story, he believed her and was furious with Joseph. He did not even listen to Joseph's part of the story. Potiphar sent Joseph to prison without any trial. After all, Joseph was only a slave and was not entitled to any trial.

Joseph was jailed for an offense that he did not commit. The LORD was with Joseph even when he was in the prison. Joseph's Godly character and attitude caught the attention of the prison guard. The prison guard unofficially promoted Joseph to be the person in charge of the prison.

The phrase 'the LORD was with Joseph' was mentioned twice in this passage. This phrase will be mentioned again and again to emphasize that Joseph was a Godly man, and the LORD was always there to protect and prosper him even through trials, temptations, and adversity.

The LORD was with Joseph every day. He walked with the LORD and obeyed the LORD. Is the LORD with you every day? Are you walking with the LORD? Are you obedient to the LORD?

Joseph had a good testimony. Potiphar and the prison guard saw that Joseph was a godly man. They saw the presence of The LORD in him. Do you have a good testimony? Will other people see Christ in you? You may be the only Bible that people will ever read!

Joseph found himself alone with Mrs. Potiphar and he was framed. It is never wise to be alone with someone of the opposite sex. Always find another person to be there as a chaperone.

The best defence against temptation is to run! Listen to Paul's advice in 1 Corinthians 10:13.

1 Corinthians 10:13, *"No temptation has taken you except what is common to man. God is faithful, who will not allow you to be tempted above what you are able but will with the temptation also make the way of escape, that you may be able to endure it."*

Application

Genesis 39 continues the story of Joseph by exploring his time spent living at Potiphar's house and subsequent imprisonment. Here are some applications from this chapter:

Integrity in the face of temptation

Joseph's refusal to succumb to Potiphar's wife's advances is evidence of his moral integrity and resolve despite persistent temptation.

Whenever faced with temptation, depend on your faith and principles for strength. Recognize the value in upholding integrity even when it can be challenging or costly.

Faithfulness at all times

Joseph's unwavering loyalty in Potiphar's house and later in prison demonstrates the importance of staying faithful in every situation.

Be consistent and dedicated to your responsibilities, regardless of your circumstances, knowing that God will acknowledge and reward your efforts.

God's presence in adversity

Joseph experienced God's favor even during the most trying of circumstances.

Remember that God is always with you, even during the most challenging moments. Seek His guidance and strength as you make decisions for the best outcome of every situation.

Integrity's Impression on others

Joseph's honesty and dedication earned him the respect of both Potiphar and the prison warden. This shows how powerfully his actions impacted those around him.

Consider how your actions and decisions affect others, and try to live in a way that positively influences and inspires.

Trusting in God's timing

Joseph experienced many setbacks on his journey, yet every step was part of God's greater plan for his life. Trusting in the timing is essential to reaching your desired destination.

Be patient and trust in God's timing even when things seem to be going wrong. Trust that He is working for your good and His glory.

Responding to false allegations

Joseph responded to false accusations with dignity and trust in God instead of reacting with anger or bitterness.

When accused or misunderstood, respond with grace and trust in God for vindication. Be wary of taking revenge or resorting to violence as this will undermine your integrity.

Studying Genesis 39 can help you trust God's presence and timing on your faith journey.

Prayer

Heavenly Father, thank You for speaking to us today. Help us to walk with You every day in obedience and submission. Help us to find favor before You and before men. We pray that Your presence will be with us through good times and bad times, in Jesus' name, Amen.

Genesis 40
Use your spiritual gifts to help others

Joseph was demoted from Potiphar's house to the prison, but the LORD was with him and prospered him. The prison warden trusted Joseph and made him the person in charge of prison affairs. God gave Joseph the gift of prophecy and dream interpretation. He interpreted the dreams of the chief cupbearer and the chief baker accurately and spot on.

Verses 1-8, *1 After these things, the butler of the king of Egypt and his baker offended their lord, the king of Egypt. 2 Pharaoh was angry with his two officers, the chief cup bearer and the chief baker. 3 He put them in custody in the house of the captain of the guard, into the prison, the place where Joseph was bound. 4 The captain of the guard assigned them to Joseph, and he took care of them. They stayed in prison many days. 5 They both dreamed a dream, each man his dream, in one night, each man according to the interpretation of his dream, the cup bearer and the baker of the king of Egypt, who were bound in the prison. 6 Joseph came in to them in the morning, and saw them, and saw that they were sad. 7 He asked Pharaoh's officers who were with him in custody in his master's house, saying, "Why do you look so sad today?" 8 They said to him, "We have dreamed a dream, and there is no one who can interpret it." Joseph said to them, "Don't interpretations belong to God? Please tell it to me."*

Reflection

'After these things' is a time marker between Genesis 39 and Genesis 40. Pharaoh was angry with his chief cupbearer and chief baker for something that they had committed. He threw them into the prison while investigations were ongoing. The chief prison guard assigned them under Joseph's care.

One night, both had a dream, and they were sad and downcast. The next morning, Joseph asked them why they were so sad and downcast. They replied that they had dreams and could not understand what they meant. Even before hearing further, Joseph declared that God could interpret their dreams for them.

Verses 9-15, *9 The chief cup bearer told his dream to Joseph, and said to him, "In my dream, behold, a vine was in front of me, 10 and in the vine were three branches. It was as though it budded, it blossomed, and its clusters produced ripe grapes. 11 Pharaoh's cup was in my hand; and I took the grapes, and pressed them into Pharaoh's cup, and I gave the cup into Pharaoh's hand." 12 Joseph said to him, "This is its interpretation: the three branches are three days. 13 Within three more days, Pharaoh will lift up your head, and restore you to your office. You will give Pharaoh's cup into his hand, the way you did when you were his cup bearer. 14 But remember me when it is well with you. Please show kindness to me, and make mention of me to Pharaoh, and bring me out of this house. 15 For indeed, I was stolen away out of the land of the Hebrews, and here also I have done nothing that they should put me into the dungeon."*

Reflection

The chief cupbearer told his dream to Joseph. In his dream, he was holding a vine with three branches that budded, bloomed, and produced grapes. He pressed the grapes into Pharoah's cup and he drank from it. Joseph replied that the three branches represent three days. Within three days, Pharoah would restore him back to be his chief cupbearer.

Joseph told him not to forget about him when he was restored to office. Joseph sought his assistance to clear his name before Pharoah. Joseph told him that he was a Hebrew slave falsely charged and imprisoned for an offense that he did not commit.

Verses 16-19, *16 When the chief baker saw that the interpretation was good, he said to Joseph, "I also was in my dream, and behold, three baskets of white bread were on my head. 17 In the uppermost basket there were all kinds of baked food for Pharaoh, and the birds ate them out of the basket on my head." 18 Joseph answered, "This is its interpretation. The three baskets are three days. 19 Within three more days, Pharaoh will lift up your head from off you, and will hang you on a tree; and the birds will eat your flesh from off you."*

Reflection

Upon hearing this, the chief baker told Joseph his dream. In the dream, he had three baskets on his head. The uppermost basket had all kinds of bread, but the birds came and ate them all. Joseph replied that the three baskets represented three days. In three days, Pharoah would order him to be hung on a tree and the birds would eat his flesh.

Verses 20-23, *20 On the third day, which was Pharaoh's birthday, he made a feast for all his servants, and he lifted up the head of the chief cup bearer and the head of the chief baker among his servants. 21 He restored the chief cup bearer to his position again, and he gave the cup into Pharaoh's hand; 22 but he hanged the chief baker, as Joseph had interpreted to them. 23 Yet the chief cup bearer didn't remember Joseph but forgot him.*

Reflection

Sure enough, Joseph's interpretation of the dreams came true to the exact detail. On the third day, Pharaoh celebrated his birthday with a grand feast. He restored the chief cupbearer to his former position but hanged the chief baker. However, the chief cupbearer forgot about Joseph and did not plead his case to Pharaoh!

Joseph acknowledged the LORD as the interpreter of the dreams. He gave all the credit to God. He did not boast about his ability. Did you a give all glory and honour to the LORD? The Christian life is all about Him and not about us.

If you are successful in your career, you will face temptations. This is when you must be extra careful. You need to walk humbly before the LORD and be obedient to His calling.

Application

Genesis 40 describes Joseph's interactions with Pharaoh's cupbearer and baker while imprisoned together. Joseph interpreted their dreams, which eventually led to his rise to power. Here are some implications from this chapter.

Use your spiritual gifts to help others

Joseph used his gift of dream interpretation to help the cupbearer and baker even when he was imprisoned. This shows the significance of using your gifts to serve others.

Recognize your spiritual gifts and look for ways to use them to serve others around you, even during difficult times. Find ways to provide comfort and assistance.

Trust in God's timing and plan

Joseph trusted in God even when his situations seem stagnant. Even after helping the cupbearer, Joseph remained in prison for another two years before being remembered and chosen to interpret Pharaoh's dreams. Joseph trusted in God's timing when his situation seemed hopeless.

Stay patient and trust that God has a plan for your life. When delays or setbacks occur, take comfort knowing that His timing is perfect and working toward your benefit.

Maintain faith in adversity

Joseph displayed unwavering faith and devotion during his imprisonment.

Keep a positive outlook and strong work ethic, even in adverse circumstances. Your dedication may open doors of opportunity that would otherwise go unrealized.

Understanding and responding to God's messages

Joseph correctly interpreted the dreams of the cupbearer and the baker.

Keep connected to God through prayer, scripture reading, and spiritual discernment. Be open to His guidance and prepared to act on what He shows you.

Remarks on gratitude and remembrance

The baker had initially failed to express his gratitude to Joseph after he was pardoned and restored. He did not honor Joseph who had assisted him.

Practice gratitude and express appreciation to those who have given you support or assistance. Make it a point to thank those you can.

Hope and perseverance

Joseph's story in this chapter is one of hope and perseverance despite prolonged imprisonment; nonetheless, he maintained a positive attitude and persevered through their challenges.

In difficult times, have faith, keep going, and trust that God has a plan for your journey. Perseverance will bring you breakthrough.

Reflecting on Genesis 40 can motivate you to utilize your spiritual gifts, have faith in God's timing, stay devoted in times of difficulty, seek His guidance, cultivate gratitude, and maintain hope and perseverance in all circumstances.

Prayer

Heavenly Father, thank You for spiritual gifts. We give You all glory, honour, and power. Without You, we can do nothing. It is all about You, and nothing is about us. You must increase, and we must decrease, in Jesus' name, Amen.

Genesis 41

From rags to fame

Meanwhile, Joseph continued to languish in prison for two more years until Pharoah had a dream and the chief cupbearer remembered him again. He interpreted Pharoah's dream and Pharoah was so impressed that he promoted him to become the second in command, equivalent to a modern-day Prime Minister. Joseph was promoted from prisoner to prime minister literally overnight.

Verses 1-8, *1 At the end of two full years, Pharaoh dreamed, and behold, he stood by the river. 2 Behold, seven cattle came up out of the river. They were sleek and fat, and they fed in the marsh grass. 3 Behold, seven other cattle came up after them out of the river, ugly and thin, and stood by the other cattle on the brink of the river. 4 The ugly and thin cattle ate up the seven sleek and fat cattle. So Pharaoh awoke. 5 He slept and dreamed a second time; and behold, seven heads of grain came up on one stalk, healthy and good. 6 Behold, seven heads of grain, thin and blasted with the east wind, sprung up after them. 7 The thin heads of grain swallowed up the seven healthy and full ears. Pharaoh awoke, and behold, it was a dream. 8 In the morning, his spirit was troubled, and he sent and called for all of Egypt's magicians and wise men. Pharaoh told them about his dreams, but no one could interpret them to Pharaoh.*

Reflection

After two long years, God planted a dream into Pharoah's sleep. In his dream, he saw seven fat and beautiful cows and seven thin and ugly cows side by side on the River Nile eating grass. The thin cows came over and ate the fat cows and he awoke. He went back to sleep and had another dream. This time, he saw seven heads of healthy and good grain arise from the ground out of a single stalk. After this, seven heads of thin and blasted grain arise from a single stack side by side. The thin heads of grain ate up the healthy heads of grain.

Pharoah awoke and was terrified. He summoned all his wise men and magicians and told them to interpret his dreams but none of them could do it.

Cows were sacred animals in Egypt because they worshiped them. Cow was a religious symbol. Grain was an economic symbol and food for local consumption and export.

Verses 8-15, *9 Then the chief cup bearer spoke to Pharaoh, saying, "I remember my faults today. 10 Pharaoh was angry with his servants and put me in custody in the house of the captain of the guard, with the chief baker. 11 We dreamed a dream in one night, he and I. Each man dreamed according to the interpretation of his dream. 12 There was with us there a young man, a Hebrew, servant to the captain of the guard, and we told him, and he interpreted to us our dreams. He interpreted to each man according to his dream. 13 As he interpreted to us, so it was. He restored me to my office, and he hanged him." 14 Then Pharaoh sent and called Joseph, and they brought him hastily out of the dungeon. He shaved himself, changed his clothing, and came in to Pharaoh. 15 Pharaoh said to Joseph, "I have dreamed a dream, and there is no one who can interpret it. I have heard it said of you, that when you hear a dream, you can interpret it."*

Reflection

The cupbearer confessed to Pharoah that he had hidden something from Pharoah. He told Pharoah that 2 years ago, he met a Hebrew slave in the prison who interpreted his dream and the late chief baker's dream, and they both came to pass. He was reinstated and later the chief baker was hanged.

Upon hearing this, Pharoah summoned Joseph from the prison to appear before him in the palace. Joseph shaved, wore new clothes, and appeared to Pharoah. Pharoah said that he had dreams that no one could interpret, and he had heard from his chief cupbearer about Joseph's ability to interpret dreams.

Verses 16-24, *16 Joseph answered Pharaoh, saying, "It isn't in me. God will give Pharaoh an answer of peace." 17 Pharaoh spoke to Joseph, "In my dream, behold, I stood on the brink of the river; 18 and behold, seven fat and sleek cattle came up out of the river. They fed in the marsh grass; 19 and behold, seven other cattle came up after them, poor and very ugly and thin, such as I never saw in all the land of Egypt for ugliness. 20 The thin and ugly cattle ate up the first seven fat cattle; 21 and when they had eaten them up, it couldn't be known that they had eaten them, but they were still ugly, as at the beginning. So I awoke. 22 I saw in my dream, and behold, seven heads of grain came up on one stalk, full and good; 23 and behold, seven heads of grain, withered, thin, and blasted with the east wind, sprung up after them. 24 The thin heads of grain swallowed up the seven good heads of grain. I told it to the magicians, but there was no one who could explain it to me."*

Reflection

Even before hearing Pharoah's dream, Joseph immediately declared that God could interpret Pharaoh's dreams. He had such great confidence in the LORD because he was walking with the LORD. He assured that the LORD would give Pharaoh peace of mind. Pharoah related his dreams to Joseph but added that when the thin cows ate the fat cows they remained just as thin. When the thin grains ate the fat grains, they were just as thin and unhealthy.

Verses 25-32, *25 Joseph said to Pharaoh, "The dream of Pharaoh is one. What God is about to do he has declared to Pharaoh. 26 The seven good cattle are seven years, and the seven good heads of grain are seven years. The dream is one. 27 The seven thin and ugly cattle that came up after them are seven years, and also the seven empty heads of grain blasted with the east wind; they will be seven years of famine. 28 That is the thing which I have spoken to Pharaoh. God has shown Pharaoh what he is about to do. 29 Behold, seven years of great plenty throughout all the land of Egypt are coming. 30 Seven years of famine will arise after them, and all the plenty will be forgotten in the land of Egypt. The famine will consume the land, 31 and the plenty will not be known in the land by reason of that famine which follows; for it will be very grievous. 32 The dream was doubled to Pharaoh, because the thing is established by God, and God will shortly bring it to pass.*

Reflection

Joseph replied that Pharoah's dreams were one dream repeated in a couplet pattern to show that the dreams were from God and would come to pass very soon. The seven fat cows and seven healthy heads of grains represented seven years of plenty. The seven thin and unhealthy heads of grains represented seven years of famine.

Egypt would experience seven years of rapid economic growth followed by seven years of severe economic recession. God repeated the same dream twice to emphasize that this event will definitely come to pass.

Verses 33-36, *33 "Now, therefore, let Pharaoh look for a discreet and wise man, and set him over the land of Egypt. 34 Let Pharaoh do this, and let him appoint overseers over the land, and take up the fifth part of the land of Egypt's produce in the seven plenteous years. 35 Let them gather all the food of these good years that come, and store grain under the hand of Pharaoh for food in the cities and let them keep it. 36 The food will be to supply the land against the seven years of famine, which will be in the land of Egypt; so that the land will not perish through the famine."*

Reflection

Joseph not only interpreted the dreams, but he also advised Pharoah on what he should do to avert disaster. He told Pharoah to appoint a capable, honest, and wise leader to manage the economy during the seven years of rapid economic growth. Taxation should be increased to 20% during the economic boom. The extra income should be kept under lock and key for use during the next seven years of recession.

Verses 37-42, *37 The thing was good in the eyes of Pharaoh, and in the eyes of all his servants. 38 Pharaoh said to his servants, "Can we find such a one as this, a man in whom is the Spirit of God?" 39 Pharaoh said to Joseph, "Because God has shown you all of this, there is no one so discreet and wise as you. 40 You shall be over my house. All my people will be ruled according to your word. Only in the throne, I will be greater than you." 41 Pharaoh said to Joseph, "Behold, I have set you over all the land of Egypt." 42 Pharaoh took off his signet ring from his hand, and put it on Joseph's hand, and arrayed him in robes of fine linen, and put a gold chain about his neck.*

Reflection

Pharoah was extremely happy with this proposal. He saw that Joseph was a Godly man who was filled with the Holy Spirit. Pharoah offered Joseph the post of Prime Minister! Joseph never expected this, not in his wildest dreams! All he expected was just a pardon and release from jail.

Pharoah gave Joseph a signet ring, robed him in the finest attire, and put a gold chain over his neck. The signet ring was a ring of authority from Pharoah. With the signet ring, Joseph could transact any business on behalf of Pharoah.

Verses 43-45, *43 He made him ride in the second chariot which he had. They cried before him, "Bow the knee!" He set him over all the land of Egypt. 44 Pharaoh said to Joseph, "I am Pharaoh. Without you, no man shall lift up his hand or his foot in all the land of Egypt." 45 Pharaoh called Joseph's name Zaphenath-Paneah. He gave him Asenath, the daughter of Potiphera priest of On as a wife. Joseph went out over the land of Egypt.*

Reflection

Joseph rode on Pharoah's royal chariot throughout the land of Egypt and the people bowed down to him in submission. Pharaoh gave Joseph an Egyptian name Zaphenath-Paneah and gave Asenath, daughter of Potiphera, priest of On, to be his wife. Joseph was transformed from a prisoner to a Prime Minister overnight because the LORD was with him. He rose from rags to fame overnight.

Verses 46-52, 46 Joseph was thirty years old when he stood before Pharaoh king of Egypt. Joseph went out from the presence of Pharaoh and went throughout all the land of Egypt. 47 In the seven plenteous years the earth produced abundantly. 48 He gathered up all the food of the seven years which were in the land of Egypt and laid up the food in the cities. He stored food in each city from the fields around that city. 49 Joseph laid up grain as the sand of the sea, very much, until he stopped counting, for it was without number. 50 To Joseph were born two sons before the year of famine came, whom Asenath, the daughter of Potiphera priest of On, bore to him. 51 Joseph called the name of the firstborn Manasseh "For", he said, "God has made me forget all my toil and all my father's house." 52 The name of the second, he called Ephraim: "For God has made me fruitful in the land of my affliction."

Reflection

Joseph was thirty years old when he became Prime Minister of Egypt. He waited thirteen years as a slave waiting upon the Lord, away from the limelight, under the LORD's training. Joseph managed the economy during the boom and stored an immense amount of grains in all the cities of Egypt. Joseph had 2 sons before the famine started, and he called them Manasseh and Ephraim. Manasseh in Hebrews means forget. Ephraim in Hebrews means fruitful.

Verses 53-57, 53 The seven years of plenty, that were in the land of Egypt, came to an end. 54 The seven years of famine began to come, just as Joseph had said. There was a famine in all lands, but in all the land of Egypt, there was bread. 55 When all the land of Egypt was famished, the people cried to Pharaoh for bread, and Pharaoh said to all the Egyptians, "Go to Joseph. What he says to you, do." 56 The famine was over all the surface of the earth. Joseph opened all the store houses and sold to the Egyptians. The famine was severe in the land of Egypt. 57 All countries came into Egypt, to Joseph, to buy grain, because the famine was severe in all the earth.

Reflection

The seven years of economic boom ended, and the seven years of economic recession started. The Egyptians from all over Egypt came to Joseph to buy grains. Very soon, the famine went global and people from all over the known world traveled to Egypt to buy grains.

Joseph gave all the glory and honour to God. Joseph knew who he was. God interpreted Pharoah's dream using Joseph as a human instrument. Did you give all the glory and honor to God?

Joseph was very humble. He willingly interpreted the dreams as prompted by the Holy Spirit without dictating any terms to Pharoah.

After 13 years of hardship, waiting in isolation and seclusion, God elevated Joseph to the second-highest position in Egypt! Joseph was under God's training for 13 years. Perhaps, you are in the same position as Joseph. Do not throw in the towel. God may be testing, growing, maturing, and training you in righteousness. God will elevate you according to His divine plan and timetable if you are faithful and obedient.

The principle of bull and bear market still applies today. In any economy, there will be bull markets and bear markets. An economic boom is always followed by a recession. You should keep adequate savings during the good time to shelter against the bad times. Times are hard during the current pandemic. If you have saved up for rainy days, you will have no problems now.

Application

Genesis 41 of Genesis depicts Joseph interpreting Pharaoh's dreams and eventually being elevated to an influential position within Egypt. Here are a few takeaways from this chapter.

God knows exactly when and how He'll provide.

Joseph became powerful after enduring years of struggle and waiting. This shows that God's timing is perfect. God uses the challenges you face to prepare and position you for the specific roles He has planned for you in His overall plan.

Be patient, trusting that God is providing for you now and in the future. Think about how your current experiences may be shaping you for new opportunities and responsibilities ahead.

Utilize spiritual gifts for His glory

Joseph utilized his spiritual gift of dream interpretation to serve others and bring glory to God.

To make a meaningful impact that aligns with God's purposes, start by recognizing your spiritual gifts and finding ways to use them to serve others and bring glory to Him.

Wisdom and discernment

Joseph showed great wisdom and discernment by not only understanding his dreams, but also coming up with a practical plan to save Egypt from a coming famine.

Pray for wisdom and discernment when making decisions. Seek guidance from God when creating plans or solving problems, and be proactive about finding practical solutions.

Humility and faithfulness

Joseph never failed to remain humble and grateful when it came to giving credit for his abilities to God.

Maintain humility, acknowledging that your gifts and successes come from God alone. Remain faithful at all times, giving Him all the credit for your achievements.

Stewardship Is the key

Joseph's wise management and stewardship of Egypt's resources was crucial for its survival during the famine.

Be wise with the resources and opportunities God has given you. Plan ahead so that you can provide for yourself and others when needed.

Responding to opportunities

Joseph was prepared and confident in God's provision when Pharoah promoted him so suddenly. He took advantage of the opportunity presented to him and fulfilled his role successfully.

Prepare yourself for opportunities by expanding your skills and faith. When opportunities present themselves, trust God and move forward with confidence.

Reconciliation is the key

Joseph's rise in status allowed him to show his family the importance of forgiveness and God's plan for reconciliation.

Think about where you need to forgive and make amends in your life, believing that God can bring healing and restoration from tough situations.

Faith during adversity

Joseph's unwavering faith throughout his trials ultimately played a crucial role in fulfilling God's plan, demonstrating the importance of maintaining faith during difficult times.

Trust that God is working behind the scenes and your faithfulness will be rewarded in challenging times.

Reflecting on Genesis 41 can be a powerful source of guidance for your life. It teaches you to have patience, humility, wisdom, and faith. You should recognize God's involvement in every situation and use your gifts for His purposes.

Prayer

Heavenly Father, we confess that we are sinners. Forgive and have mercy on us. Thank You for justification, salvation, and eternal life. Help us to save up for rainy days so that we will be able to cope when the bad times arrive. We give you all glory, power, and honour, in Jesus' name, Amen.

Genesis 42

God's provision in famine

The camera angle shifted back from Joseph in Egypt to Jacob and his sons in Canaan. The economic recession was hitting hard and there was insufficient food in Canaan. When Jacob heard that there was food for sale in Egypt, he summoned his sons for an urgent meeting.

Verses 1-5, *1 Now Jacob saw that there was grain in Egypt, and Jacob said to his sons, "Why do you look at one another?" 2 He said, "Behold, I have heard that there is grain in Egypt. Go down there, and buy for us from there, so that we may live, and not die." 3 Joseph's ten brothers went down to buy grain from Egypt. 4 But Jacob didn't send Benjamin, Joseph's brother, with his brothers; for he said, "Lest perhaps harm happen to him." 5 The sons of Israel came to buy among those who came, for the famine was in the land of Canaan.*

Reflection

Jacob commanded his sons to go down to Egypt to buy grains to survive the famine. Jacob sent ten of his sons to Egypt but he did not allow Benjamin to go along in case some mishap might happen to Benjamin. He had already lost Joseph and he could not afford to lose Benjamin. These were his two youngest sons by Rachel, the wife that he loved the most.

Verses 6-9, *6 Joseph was the governor over the land. It was he who sold to all the people of the land. Joseph's brothers came and bowed themselves down to him with their faces to the earth. 7 Joseph saw his brothers, and he recognized them, but acted like a stranger to them, and spoke roughly with them. He said to them, "Where did you come from?" They said, "From the land of Canaan, to buy food." 8 Joseph recognized his brothers, but they didn't recognize him. 9 Joseph remembered the dreams which he dreamed about them, and said to them, "You are spies! You have come to see the nakedness of the land."*

Reflection

Joseph was the prime minister of Egypt. Everyone who wanted grain had to buy from Joseph. Joseph's brothers came before Joseph and bowed before him. This was a fulfillment of Joseph's dream, Genesis 37:7. Joseph recognized his brothers, but they did not recognize him.

The last time they saw Joseph was 20 years ago and he was now dressed as a high-ranking Egyptian official. Joseph spoke to them harshly asking where they were from. They replied that they were from Canaan and had come to buy grains. Joseph accused them of espionage.

Genesis 37:7, *"for behold, we were binding sheaves in the field, and behold, my sheaf arose and also stood upright; and behold, your sheaves came around, and bowed down to my sheaf."*

Verses 10-14, *10 They said to him, "No, my lord, but your servants have come to buy food. 11 We are all one man's sons; we are honest men. Your servants are not spies." 12 He said to them, "No, but you have come to see the nakedness of the land!" 13 They said, "We, your servants, are twelve brothers, the sons of one man in the land of Canaan; and behold, the youngest is today with our father, and one is no more." 14 Joseph said to them, "It is like I told you, saying, 'You are spies!'*

Reflection

They replied that they were not spies. They clarified that their father and their youngest brother were in Canaan and one of their brothers was not with them anymore. Joseph continued to accuse them of espionage. He wanted to test their level of honesty and integrity.

Verses 15-19, *15 By this you shall be tested. By the life of Pharaoh, you shall not go out from here, unless your youngest brother comes here. 16 Send one of you and let him get your brother, and you shall be bound, that your words may be tested, whether there is truth in you, or else by the life of Pharaoh surely you are spies." 17 He put them all together into custody for three days. 18 Joseph said to them the third day, "Do this, and live, for I fear God. 19 If you are honest men, then let one of your brothers be bound in your prison; but you go, carry grain for the famine of your houses.*

Reflection

Joseph gave them an ultimatum to bring Benjamin to Egypt, otherwise he would not see them again. Joseph imprisoned them for three days. On the third day, he released them but demanded that one of them be jailed as collateral until Benjamin was brought to him.

Verses 20-22, *20 Bring your youngest brother to me; so will your words be verified, and you won't die." They did so. 21 They said to one another, "We are certainly guilty concerning our brother, in that we saw the distress of his soul when he begged us, and we wouldn't listen. Therefore, this distress has come upon us." 22*

Reuben answered them, saying, "Didn't I tell you, saying, 'Don't sin against the child,' and you wouldn't listen? Therefore also, behold, his blood is required."

Reflection

Joseph commanded his brothers to take the grains to Canaan and come back with their youngest brother. The brothers admitted their guilt for selling Joseph to the Ishmaelite slave traders twenty years ago. Their guilt had come back to haunt them now. Rueben tried to vindicate himself by saying that he was not in favour of selling Joseph to the slave traders.

Verses 23-28, *23 They didn't know that Joseph understood them; for there was an interpreter between them. 24 He turned himself away from them and wept. Then he returned to them, and spoke to them, and took Simeon from among them, and bound him before their eyes. 25 Then Joseph gave a command to fill their bags with grain, and to restore each man's money into his sack, and to give them food for the way. So, it was done to them. 26 They loaded their donkeys with their grain and departed from there. 27 As one of them opened his sack to give his donkey food in the lodging place, he saw his money. Behold, it was in the mouth of his sack. 28 He said to his brothers, "My money is restored! Behold, it is in my sack!" Their hearts failed them, and they turned trembling to one another, saying, "What is this that God has done to us?"*

Reflection

Joseph understood what they said but he pretended as though he did not. He turned aside and wept. When he returned, he took Simeon and chained him in front of his brothers. Joseph commanded his workers to fill their bags with grain, returned their money into the bags, and sent them off on the way.

When they reached the lodging place and opened one of the bags, they saw the money and were terrified. They feared for their lives as Joseph might come with his army and arrest them for theft.

Verses 29-34, *29 They came to Jacob their father, to the land of Canaan, and told him all that had happened to them, saying, 30 "The man, the lord of the land, spoke roughly with us, and took us for spies of the country. 31 We said to him, 'We are honest men. We are no spies. 32 We are twelve brothers, sons of our father; one is no more, and the youngest is today with our father in the land of Canaan.' 33 The man, the lord of the land, said to us, 'By this, I will know that you are honest men: leave one of your brothers with me, and take grain for the famine of your houses, and go your way. 34 Bring your youngest brother to me. Then I will know that you are not spies, but that you are honest men. So, I will deliver your brother to you, and you shall trade in the land.'"*

Reflection

They returned to Canaan and told Jacob how a high-ranking Egyptian treated them harshly and accused them of espionage. They related how they were questioned until they said their father and youngest brother were in Canaan. Subsequently, Simeon was kept in custody until Benjamin comes to Egypt.

Verses 35-38, *35 As they emptied their sacks, behold, each man's bundle of money was in his sack. When they and their father saw their bundles of money, they were afraid. 36 Jacob, their father, said to them, "You have bereaved me of my children! Joseph is no more, Simeon is no more, and you want to take Benjamin away. All these things are against me." 37 Reuben spoke to his father, saying, "Kill my two sons, if I don't bring him to you. Entrust him to my care, and I will bring him to you again." 38 He said, "My son shall not go down with you; for his brother is dead, and he only is left. If harm happens to him along the way in which you go, then you will bring down my gray hairs with sorrow to Sheol."*

Joseph was a type of Christ. He saved the known world of his time from death. Jesus Christ saves humanity from eternal death, John 3:16.

John 3:16, *For God so loved the world, that he gave his only born Son, that whoever believes in him should not perish, but have eternal life.*

Honesty is the best policy. Because the sons of Jacob told the truth to Joseph, they were able to tell a consistent story every time they face Joseph. They were transparent before Joseph who knew everything about them. Have you come clean before Jesus? You cannot hide anything from him because He knows everything about you. Have you confessed and repented your sins to Jesus, who is omnipotent, omnipresent, and omniscient?

Application

Genesis 42 chronicles Joseph's interaction with his brothers during their famine relief trip to Egypt for grain purchases. Here are some applications from this chapter.

Facing past mistakes

Joseph's brothers learned the importance of addressing and correcting their previous mistakes when they encountered Joseph again, whom they had sold into slavery.

Apologize and make amends for past mistakes. Taking responsibility for your past actions and seeking to make amends is crucial for personal growth and reconciliation. You need to be humble and accept the consequences of your choices.

God is in control during times of trial.

God used the famine to bring Joseph's brothers to Egypt as part of His plan to bring his family together, showing how He can use difficult times to achieve His goals.

Trust in God during hard times and think about how He might be using your situation for His bigger plans.

The power of conscience

Joseph's brothers felt guilt over past actions they committed, which became apparent as they faced hardships.

Listen to your conscience and allow it to guide your behavior towards repentance and justice. When guilt arises, use it as an incentive to seek forgiveness and change your behavior.

Testing and transformation

Joseph tested his brothers to see if they had changed, highlighting the importance of testing and transformation in the process of reconciliation.

See challenges as opportunities to grow and change. But when making up with others, make sure to check if they have really changed.

Compassion and mercy

Joseph displayed grace, kindness and mercy towards his brothers despite his power over them.

Practice mercy and kindness even towards those who have wronged you. Channel God's forgiving nature into all your relationships.

Honesty Is Key

The brothers' honesty about their family situation and their younger brother Benjamin was crucial in their interactions with Joseph. Their openness helped establish trust with him.

Prioritize honesty in all your dealings. Building trust through truthful dialogue is vital to maintaining healthy relationships.

God provides in famine

God provided for Jacob's family through Joseph during their famine years, showing His providential care even during difficult times.

Trust God in times of scarcity or hardship; have faith that He will meet your needs and guide you through difficult periods.

Family reunion and reconciliation.

Joseph's story sets the scene for eventual family reconciliation and emphasizes its importance.

Focus on family unity and work toward reconciliation within your household. Seek to repair broken relationships and inculcate an atmosphere of forgiveness and love.

When thinking about Genesis 42, remember to approach your relationships and challenges with an attitude of repentance, trust in God's control, and a focus on compassion and reconciliation.

Prayer

Heavenly Father, thank You for speaking to us through Your Living Word of eternal life. Thank You for saving us from sin and death in exchange for righteousness and eternal life. We acknowledge that it is by grace that we are saved, through faith in Christ and not by work, in Jesus' name, Amen.

Genesis 43
Emotional reunion

After the brothers had returned to Canaan, Jacob refused to let Benjamin go to Egypt. Everything was put on hold for 1 whole year until the economic recession hit hard and the famine continued unabated. Even the grains that they bought from Egypt ran out. At this stage, Jacob had no choice but to send the brothers back to Egypt with Benjamin. Joseph had an emotional reunion with his brothers but did not reveal his identity.

Verses 1-5, *1 The famine was severe in the land. 2 When they had eaten up the grain which they had brought out of Egypt, their father said to them, "Go again, buy us a little more food." 3 Judah spoke to him, saying, "The man solemnly warned us, saying, 'You shall not see my face unless your brother is with you.' 4 If you'll send our brother with us, we'll go down and buy you food; 5 but if you don't send him, we won't go down, for the man said to us, 'You shall not see my face unless your brother is with you.'"*

Reflection

Jacob summoned his children to go back to Egypt to buy more grains. Judah replied that they could not go back to Egypt unless Benjamin comes along with them.

Verses 6-10, *6 Israel said, "Why did you treat me so badly, telling the man that you had another brother?" 7 They said, "The man asked directly concerning ourselves, and concerning our relatives, saying, 'Is your father still alive? Have you another brother?' We just answered his questions. Is there any way we could know that he would say, 'Bring your brother down?'" 8 Judah said to Israel, his father, "Send the boy with me, and we'll get up and go, so that we may live, and not die, both we, and you, and also our little ones. 9 I'll be collateral for him. From my hand will you require him. If I don't bring him to you and set him before you, then let me bear the blame forever; 10 for if we hadn't delayed, surely, we would have returned a second time by now."*

Reflection

Jacob censured his sons for telling the truth to the high-ranking Egyptian officer. They replied that they were not willing to tell any lie to the Egyptian officer. Judah rose up to the occasion and said that he would stand surety for the safe return of Benjamin. Should anything untoward happen to Benjamin, he was willing to pay with his life.

Verses 11-14, *11 Their father, Israel, said to them, "If it must be so, then do this: Take from the choice fruits of the land in your bags and carry down a present for the man, a little balm, a little honey, spices and myrrh, nuts, and almonds; 12 and take double money in your hand, and take back the money that was returned in the mouth of your sacks. Perhaps it was an oversight. 13 Take your brother also, get up, and return to the man. 14 May God Almighty give you mercy before the man, that he may release to you your other brother and Benjamin. If I am bereaved of my children, I am bereaved."*

Reflection

Jacob finally agreed to allow his children to go back to Egypt with Benjamin. They were to take gifts, fruits, balm, honey, spices, myrrh, nuts, and almonds, and return the money they found in their bags. Jacob prayed to God for journey mercy and protection.

Verses 15-17, *15 The men took that present, and they took double money in their hand, and Benjamin; and got up, went down to Egypt, and stood before Joseph. 16 When Joseph saw Benjamin with them, he said to the steward of his house, "Bring the men into the house, and butcher an animal, and prepare; for the men will dine with me at noon." 17 The man did as Joseph commanded, and the man brought the men to Joseph's house.*

Reflection

Jacob's sons took double the amount of money, went down to Egypt, and appeared before Joseph again. Joseph was very happy to see his younger brother Benjamin. He instructed his staff to bring his brothers to his residence to have a luncheon with him.

Verses 18-22, *18 The men were afraid because they were brought to Joseph's house; and they said, "Because of the money that was returned in our sacks the first time, we're brought in; that he may seek occasion against us, attack us, and seize us as slaves, along with our donkeys." 19 They came near to the steward of Joseph's house, and they spoke to him at the door of the house, 20 and said, "Oh, my lord, we indeed came down the first time to buy food. 21 When we came to the lodging place, we opened our sacks, and behold, each man's money was in the mouth of his sack, our money in full weight. We have brought it back in our hand. 22 We have brought down other money in our hand to buy food. We don't know who put our money in our sacks."*

Reflection

The brothers were terrified that Joseph might be planning to harm them. On nearing Joseph's residence, they told Joseph's steward that they paid for the grains on their last visit but the money mysteriously reappeared in their bags. They could not explain how this could have happened.

Verses 23-25, *23 He said, "Peace be to you. Don't be afraid. Your God, and the God of your father, has given you treasure in your sacks. I received your money." He brought Simeon out to them. 24 The man brought the men into Joseph's house and gave them water, and they washed their feet. He gave their donkeys fodder. 25 They prepared the present for Joseph's coming at noon, for they heard that they should eat bread there.*

Reflection

The steward reassured them that everything was in order. He had received the payment in full. The steward was aware that Joseph had deliberately returned their money to them in secret. He replied that their God might have done a miracle to help them financially.

Verses 26-29, *26 When Joseph came home, they brought him the present which was in their hand into the house and bowed themselves down to the earth before him. 27 He asked them of their welfare, and said, "Is your father well, the old man of whom you spoke? Is he yet alive?" 28 They said, "Your servant, our father, is well. He is still alive." They bowed down humbly. 29 He lifted up his eyes, and saw Benjamin, his brother, his mother's son, and said, "Is this your youngest brother, of whom you spoke to me?" He said, "God be gracious to you, my son."*

Reflection

When Joseph came home, his brothers took out their presents and bowed down before him, fulfilling again the prophecy of Joseph's dream. Joseph asked them whether their father was still alive. They replied that Jacob was still alive. When Joseph saw his biological brother Benjamin, he was visibly touched. He inquired whether he was indeed Benjamin and spoke graciously to him.

Verses 30-34, *30 Joseph hurried, for his heart yearned over his brother; and he sought a place to weep. He entered into his room and wept there. 31 He washed his face and came out. He controlled himself, and said, "Serve the meal." 32 They served him by himself, and them by themselves, and the Egyptians who ate with him by themselves, because the Egyptians don't eat with the Hebrews, for that is an abomination to the Egyptians. 33 They sat before him, the firstborn according to his birthright, and the youngest according to his youth, and the men marveled with one another. 34 He sent portions to them from before him, but Benjamin's portion was five times as much as any of theirs. They drank and were merry with him.*

Reflection

Joseph could not contain his emotion any longer. He entered his room and wept uncontrollably. Joseph made his brothers sit in chronological order from the eldest to the youngest. The brothers were spellbound wondering how Joseph knew their chronological ages. They did not suspect that Joseph was indeed their brother. They might have expected Joseph to be in Egypt as a slave but certainly not as the Prime Minister of Egypt!

Judah was a type of Christ. He stood as collateral for Benjamin. Should anything untoward happen to Benjamin, he was willing to die in his place. Jesus stood as collateral for you and me. He willingly died in our place to take our sins upon Himself. He died so that we may live.

The brother's reunion was the result of God's providence and fulfillment of divine prophecy. God sent Joseph to Egypt to make the way for his family to move out of Canaan to Egypt. God's plan unfolded behind the scene throughout history.

God scripted your life story in accordance with His divine plan. When you look back into your life story, you will see God's providence at work. After all, history is His story.

Application

Genesis 43 continues the story of Joseph and his brothers' second journey to Egypt.

Courage to face challenges

Jacob and his sons faced the difficult decision of returning to Egypt despite their fear and uncertainties. They needed courage to do this task.

When confronted with obstacles, pray for courage and take bold steps forward. Trust that God will provide the strength and guidance you require to overcome them.

Responsibility and sacrifice

Judah took charge for Benjamin's safety, showing a willingness to sacrifice himself in his brother's best interest. This illustrates the significance of taking responsibility and making sacrifices for others.

Reflect on the areas in your relationships where you can take more responsibility and make sacrifices for the well-being of your partner, to demonstrate love and commitment.

Trusting in God's Provision

Despite their fears, Jacob and his sons relied on God to provide food and protection during a period of famine. And their faith was rewarded with food and favor from above.

Trust God in times of scarcity or uncertainty in your own life. Pray for His guidance, believing He will provide for all your needs.

Reconciliation and forgiveness

Joseph's continued kindness toward his brothers despite their past actions demonstrates both forgiveness and reconciliation as powerful forces for change.

If there are broken relationships in your life, take steps towards reconciliation. Offer forgiveness and strive to restore harmony.

Generosity and hospitality.

Joseph's generosity towards his brothers, like the feast he hosted, highlights the significance of being generous and hospitable, even towards those who had harmed you in the past.

Be generous and kind in everything you do. Welcome others with open arms, sharing resources freely and showing kindness even to those who may not deserve it.

God Is Present In Difficult Situations

God was evident in how Joseph's brothers were treated in Egypt, showing His hand at work even during difficult circumstances.

Look for signs of God's presence in tough times and believe that He is working for your good, even if it's hard to see.

Honesty and Integrity

The brother's honesty in returning the silver they found in their sacks showed their integrity and desire to do what was right.

Prioritize honesty and integrity in everything that you do. Be truthful and transparent even when difficult; strive to do what is right in every circumstance.

Love and Commitment to Family Life

The dedication of Benjamin's brothers to his well-being demonstrates the importance of family love and loyalty.

Support and prioritize each other to build a loving and committed family. Work together to overcome challenges.

Lessons from Genesis 43 can help guide you to live with courage, responsibility, trust in God's provision, generosity, honesty, and a strong commitment to family.

Prayer

Heavenly Father, thank you for scripting out the story of our lives through our life events.

Thank You for looking after us throughout our lives. Thank You for divine protection, provision, guidance, health, friends, and family. Thank You for sending Jesus Christ to be an atoning sacrifice for our sins, in Jesus' name, Amen.

Genesis 44

Forgiveness and reconciliation

In the second year of the famine, the brothers came back to Egypt and bowed their knees before Joseph with gifts and money to buy more grains. Joseph tested them by secretly returning each person's money into their bags and planting his silver cup in Benjamin's sack. After they had left his residence, he sent his steward to inspect their bags and found the silver cup in Benjamin's bag.

Verses 1-6, *1 He commanded the steward of his house, saying, "Fill the men's sacks with food, as much as they can carry, and put each man's money in his sack's mouth. 2 Put my cup, the silver cup, in the sack's mouth of the youngest, with his grain money." He did according to the word that Joseph had spoken. 3 As soon as the morning was light, the men were sent away, they and their donkeys. 4 When they had gone out of the city and were not yet far off, Joseph said to his steward, "Up, follow after the men. When you overtake them, ask them, 'Why have you rewarded evil for good? 5 Isn't this that from which my lord drinks, and by which he indeed divines? You have done evil in so doing.'" 6 He overtook them, and he spoke these words to them.*

Reflection

Joseph instructed his steward to fill the brother's sack with grains and return their money. He also instructed his steward to secretly put his silver cup into Benjamin's sack. As the brother left Joseph's residence the next morning, Joseph sent his steward to overtake them and stop them in their tracks and questioned them over the loss of Joseph's silver cup.

Verses 7-10, *7 They said to him, "Why does my lord speak such words as these? Far be it from your servants that they should do such a thing! 8 Behold, the money, which we found in our sacks' mouths, we brought again to you out of the land of Canaan. How then should we steal silver or gold out of your lord's house? 9 With whomever of your servants it is found, let him die, and we also will be my lord's slaves." 10 He said, "Now also let it be according to your words. He with whom it is found will be my slave, and you will be blameless."*

Reflection

The steward accused the brothers of stealing Joseph's silver cup. The brothers replied that they had not stolen the silver cup. They permitted the steward to search them and if any stolen items were found, that person should die and the rest should be enslaved.

Verses 11-14, *11 Then they hurried, and each man took his sack down to the ground, and each man opened his sack. 12 He searched, beginning with the oldest, and ending at the youngest. The cup was found in Benjamin's sack. 13 Then they tore their clothes, and each man loaded his donkey, and returned to the city. 14 Judah and his brothers came to Joseph's house, and he was still there. They fell on the ground before him. 15 Joseph said to them, "What deed is this that you have done? Don't you know that such a man as I can indeed do divination?"*

Reflection

Upon inspection of each of the brother's bag, beginning from the eldest to the youngest, the steward found the silver cup in Benjamin's bag. In exasperation, they tore their clothes and returned to Joseph's residence.

In the custom of those days, the tearing of clothes means remorse, sorrow, or repentance. Terrified, they bowed prostrate before Joseph and pleaded before him for mercy.

Joseph interrogated them demanding an explanation. Joseph was putting them to the test. He framed them with theft to test their attitude, integrity, and character.

Verses 16-18, *16 Judah said, "What will we tell my lord? What will we speak? How will we clear ourselves? God has found out the iniquity of your servants. Behold, we are my lord's slaves, both we and he also in whose hand the cup is found." 17 He said, "Far be it from me that I should do so. The man in whose hand the cup is found, he will be my slave; but as for you, go up in peace to your father." 18 Then Judah came near to him, and said, "Oh, my lord, please let your servant speak a word in my lord's ears, and don't let your anger burn against your servant; for you are even as Pharaoh.*

Reflection

Judah rose up to the occasion again with honesty, leadership, and integrity. On behalf of his brothers, he confessed that all of them had sinned against Joseph and deserved to be his slaves, including Benjamin. In reply, Joseph said that only Benjamin would be his slave and all the brothers were free. Judah came to the rescue of Benjamin.

Verses 19-26, *19 My lord asked his servants, saying, 'Have you a father or a brother?' 20 We said to my lord, 'We have a father, an old man, and a child of his old age, a little one; and his brother is dead, and he alone is left of his mother, and his father loves him.' 21 You said to your servants, 'Bring him down to me, that I may set my eyes on him.' 22 We said to my lord, 'The boy can't leave his father, for if he should leave his father, his father would die.' 23 You said to your servants, 'Unless your youngest brother comes down with you, you will see my face no more.' 24 When we came up to your servant my father, we told him the words of my lord. 25 Our father said, 'Go again and buy us a little food.' 26 We said, 'We can't go down. If our youngest brother is with us, then we will go down: for we may not see the man's face, unless our youngest brother is with us.'*

Reflection

Addressing Joseph respectfully as his lord, Judah told him the whole story truthfully. He said that his father was an old man who loved his youngest son Benjamin very much. Another of his sons, referring to Joseph was believed to have died. His father had overprotected Benjamin and refused to be separated from him. They could not return to Egypt earlier because their father refused to released Benjamin.

Verses 27-34, *27 Your servant, my father, said to us, 'You know that my wife bore me two sons. 28 One went out from me, and I said, "Surely he is torn in pieces;" and I haven't seen him since. 29 If you take this one also from me, and harm happens to him, you will bring down my gray hairs with sorrow to Sheol.' 30 Now therefore when I come to your servant my father, and the boy is not with us; since his life is bound up in the boy's life; 31 it will happen, when he sees that the boy is no more, that he will die. Your servants will bring down the gray hairs of your servant, our father, with sorrow to Sheol. 32 For your servant became collateral for the boy to my father, saying, 'If I don't bring him to you, then I will bear the blame to my father forever.' 33 Now, therefore, please let your servant stay instead of the boy, my lord's slave; and let the boy go up with his brothers. 34 For how will I go up to my father, if the boy isn't with me?— lest I see the evil that will come on my father."*

Reflection

Judah said that his father had two sons from his favourite deceased wife Rachel. After the disappearance of the elder son, Joseph, his life was tied to the younger son, Benjamin. Should anything untoward happen to Benjamin, he would surely die too.

Judah had promised his father that he was responsible for Benjamin's safe return. He had given his life as collateral for Benjamin's life. Judah told Joseph that he would take the place of Benjamin to pay for the alleged theft of the silver cup and bear all the punishment for him.

Judah confessed his sin to Joseph on behalf of all his brothers. Have you confessed your sin to Jesus?

As mentioned before, Judah is a type of Christ, Judah stood as collateral for Benjamin. Should anything happen to Benjamin, Judah would take the punishment on Benjamin's behalf. Jesus stood as collateral for you and me. He took our sins upon Himself and paid the ultimate price to secure our forgiveness through His death on the cross.

Application

Genesis 44 tells how Joseph tested his brothers by putting a silver cup in Benjamin's sack and accusing him of stealing. This chapter highlights themes of repentance, self-sacrifice, and reconciliation; here are some applications.

Integrity is key

Integrity shines through as Joseph's brothers return willingly when accused of theft instead of abandoning Benjamin.

Commit to living your life with integrity even when it is challenging. Always be honest and accountable for your actions. Strive to do what is right and don't give in to pressure to take the easy way out.

Self-sacrifice and love

Judah's selfless act in offering himself instead of Benjamin demonstrates his profound love and commitment to his family.

Show selfless love in your relationships by putting others' needs before your own and showing genuine care and commitment.

Repentance and transformation

Joseph's brothers express remorse and actively work to make amends for their previous mistreatment of him; illustrating the possibility of personal growth and redemption.

Reflect on parts of your life where you may need to make amends and change your actions. Take steps to improve, and try to make things right with anyone you have hurt.

Testing and proving character

Joseph's test revealed the true character of his brothers.

View challenges as opportunities to grow and show your true self, and tough situations as times to strengthen and reveal true values.

Interceding for others

Judah's plea on Benjamin's behalf to Joseph shows the power of intercession.

Advocate for those in need, stand up for others, and intervene on their behalf while working for positive outcomes for the most vulnerable.

Understanding God's bigger plan

These events serve as a testament to God's larger plan in action, leading to reconciliation and protecting Jacob's family.

Trust that God has a plan for your life, even when it's not clear. Believe that He is working through your circumstances to bring about family unity and responsibility.

Family unity and responsibility

Benjamin's brothers' sense of solidarity and responsibility show us the value of standing together as a family unit.

Strengthen family bonds by sticking together during times of distress. Offer support and take ownership of one another's wellbeing.

Forgiveness and reconciliation

Joseph's ultimate aim was reconciliation between himself and his brothers, showing the power of forgiveness and healing relationships.

To have better relationships, forgive those who have hurt you and work towards restoration and renewal.

Genesis 44 teaches you about living a life of integrity, self-sacrificial love, repentance, and commitment to family unity and reconciliation.

Prayer

Heavenly Father, thank You for salvation, the forgiveness of sins, justification, and the gift of eternal life. Thank You for sending Jesus Christ to die on the cross as an atoning sacrifice for our sins, in Jesus' name, Amen.

Genesis 45

Forgiveness, and Reconciliation

After Judah's repentance, Joseph could not contain his emotion any longer. He knew that his brothers had changed. They were no longer deceitful and conniving. He saw no signs of sibling rivalries among them. Joseph revealed his identity, forgave their sins, gave them grace, and reconciled to them. Joseph sent them back to Canaan to bring their father Jacob and their whole family to Egypt.

Verses 1-4, *1 Then Joseph couldn't control himself before all those who stood before him, and he called out, "Cause everyone to go out from me!" No one else stood with him, while Joseph made himself known to his brothers. 2 He wept aloud. The Egyptians heard, and the house of Pharaoh heard. 3 Joseph said to his brothers, "I am Joseph! Does my father still live?" His brothers couldn't answer him; for they were terrified at his presence. 4 Joseph said to his brothers, "Come near to me, please." They came near. He said, "I am Joseph, your brother, whom you sold into Egypt.*

Reflection

When everyone had left the hall and Joseph was alone with his brothers, he revealed his identity to them. Joseph wept so loudly until all the Egyptians and members of Pharoah's household heard it. He called his brothers to him saying that he was Joseph whom they sold as a slave to Egypt 15 years ago. This was a very touching reunion. His brothers were dumbfounded and shocked to answer back!

Verses 5-8, *5 Now don't be grieved, nor angry with yourselves, that you sold me here, for God sent me before you to preserve life. 6 For these two years the famine has been in the land, and there are yet five years, in which there will be no plowing and no harvest. 7 God sent me before you to preserve for you a remnant in the earth, and to save you alive by a great deliverance. 8 So now it wasn't you who sent me here, but God, and he has made me a father to Pharaoh, lord of all his house, and ruler over all the land of Egypt.*

Reflection

Joseph reassured and pacified them, acknowledging God's providence for bringing him to Egypt before them to save their lives. The family would not be able to survive the famine which would last 5 more years. God was at work all the time working behind the scenes to protect them.

Verses 9-11, *9 Hurry, and go up to my father, and tell him, 'This is what your son Joseph says, "God has made me lord of all Egypt. Come down to me. Don't wait. 10 You shall dwell in the land of Goshen, and you will be near to me, you, your children, your children's children, your flocks, your herds, and all that you have. 11 There I will provide for you; for there are yet five years of famine; lest you come to poverty, you, and your household, and all that you have."'*

Reflection

Joseph told them to go back to Canaan, report everything they witnessed in Egypt, and bring their father, mothers, sisters, slaves, possessions, and livestock to Egypt. It would be a lock, stock, and barrel family migration. Joseph would give them land in Goshen and would take care of all their needs. They would be able to survive the famine in Egypt.

Verses 12-15, *12 Behold, your eyes see, and the eyes of my brother Benjamin, that it is my mouth that speaks to you. 13 You shall tell my father of all my glory in Egypt, and of all that you have seen. You shall hurry and bring my father down here." 14 He fell on his brother Benjamin's neck and wept, and Benjamin wept on his neck. 15 He kissed all his brothers and wept on them. After that, his brothers talked with him.*

Reflection

Joseph instructed his brothers to tell their father Jacob about him. They must bring Jacob to him as soon as possible. He fell on Benjamin's neck, and they wept together. He kissed all his brothers and finally, they were able to regain their composure and talk with Joseph.

Verses 16-20, *16 The report of it was heard in Pharaoh's house, saying, "Joseph's brothers have come." It pleased Pharaoh well, and his servants. 17 Pharaoh said to Joseph, "Tell your brothers, 'Do this: Load your animals, and go, travel to the land of Canaan. 18 Take your father and your households and come to me, and I will give you the good of the land of Egypt, and you will eat the fat of the land.' 19 Now you are commanded to do this: Take wagons out of the land of Egypt for your little ones, and for your wives, and bring your father, and come. 20*

Also, don't concern yourselves about your belongings, for the good of all the land of Egypt is yours."

Reflection

Pharoah intervened at this juncture and was very supportive of Joseph's plan to relocate his family to Egypt. He also supplied wagons so that Jacob and his family could travel to Egypt in comfort and luxury.

Verses 21-24, 21 The sons of Israel did so. Joseph gave them wagons, according to the commandment of Pharaoh, and gave them provisions for the way. 22 He gave each one of them changes of clothing, but to Benjamin, he gave three hundred pieces of silver and five changes of clothing. 23 He sent the following to his father: ten donkeys loaded with the good things of Egypt, and ten female donkeys loaded with grain and bread and provision for his father by the way. 24 So he sent his brothers away, and they departed. He said to them, "See that you don't quarrel on the way."

Reflection

Joseph provided his brothers with new clothes, but he gave Benjamin 300 pieces of silver and 5 sets of new clothes. By now, Joseph had become very rich, powerful, and influential. He gave special treatment to Benjamin, his biological brother. He also gave Jacob, 10 male and 10 female donkeys, grains, and bread. As they departed, Joseph warned them not to quarrel among themselves.

Verses 25-33, 25 They went up out of Egypt, and came into the land of Canaan, to Jacob their father. 26 They told him, saying, "Joseph is still alive, and he is ruler over all the land of Egypt." His heart fainted, for he didn't believe them. 27 They told him all the words of Joseph, which he had said to them. When he saw the wagons which Joseph had sent to carry him, the spirit of Jacob, their father, revived. 28 Israel said, "It is enough. Joseph my son is still alive. I will go and see him before I die."

Reflection

The brothers arrived home to Canaan and reported to Jacob as per Joseph's instructions. When Jacob saw the wagons and heard that Joseph was alive, his spirit man was rekindled. He declared that he would go to Egypt to meet his long-lost son Joseph before he dies.

Application

Joseph is a type of Christ. Christ revealed His identity to us, forgave our sins, gave us grace, and reconciled us to Him.

The story of Joseph is a story of God's providence. History is God's story. There is no accident or coincidence in God's kingdom. God orchestrated and scripted every circumstance of our lives according to His divine plan.

The story of Joseph is a picture of God's grace in our lives. Joseph forgave his brothers for selling him as a slave to Egypt. Jesus forgave us for sins against God. The penalty of sin is eternal death but Jesus gave us eternal life.

Prayer

Heavenly Father, thank You for these amazing stories in the life of Joseph. These stories are examples for us to learn and train in righteousness. Thank You for providence and grace, in Jesus' name, Amen.

Genesis 46
The joy of reconciliation

Jacob finally left Canaan and migrated to Egypt. He uprooted lock, stock, and barrel, with his wives, children, great-grandchildren, possessions, and livestock. They traveled in style, luxury, and comfort on Egyptian wagons. When Jacob finally met Joseph, their reunion was very emotional and touching.

Verses 1-4, *1 Israel traveled with all that he had, and came to Beersheba, and offered sacrifices to the God of his father, Isaac. 2 God spoke to Israel in the visions of the night, and said, "Jacob, Jacob!" He said, "Here I am." 3 He said, "I am God, the God of your father. Don't be afraid to go down into Egypt, for there I will make of you a great nation. 4 I will go down with you into Egypt. I will also surely bring you up again. Joseph's hand will close your eyes."*

The LORD appeared to Jacob in a night vision at Beersheba when he offered sacrifices to Him. The LORD called him by his old name, Jacob, twice, for emphasis. The LORD revealed to Jacob that He is the God of his father. The LORD confirmed that He is God's will and has nothing to fear. The LORD would follow him to Egypt and later bring him out from Egypt. His son Joseph would be by his side on his deathbed.

Verses 5-7, *5 Jacob rose up from Beersheba, and the sons of Israel carried Jacob, their father, their little ones, and their wives, in the wagons which Pharaoh had sent to carry him. 6 They took their livestock, and their goods, which they had gotten in the land of Canaan, and came into Egypt—Jacob, and all his offspring with him, 7 his sons, and his sons' sons with him, his daughters, and his sons' daughters, and he brought all his offspring with him into Egypt.*

Application

With this assurance, Jacob continued his journey. Soon, the whole company of Jacob's family arrived in Egypt.

Verses 8-27, *8 These are the names of the children of Israel, who came into Egypt, Jacob and his sons: Reuben, Jacob's firstborn. 9 The sons of Reuben: Hanoch, Pallu, Hezron, and Carmi. 10 The sons of Simeon: Jemuel, Jamin, Ohad, Jachin, Zohar, and Shaul the son of a Canaanite woman. 11 The sons of Levi: Gershon, Kohath, and Merari. 12 The sons of Judah: Er, Onan, Shelah,*

Perez, and Zerah; but Er and Onan died in the land of Canaan. The sons of Perez were Hezron and Hamul. 13 The sons of Issachar: Tola, Puvah, Lob, and Shimron. 14 The sons of Zebulun: Sered, Elon, and Jahleel. 15 These are the sons of Leah, whom she bore to Jacob in Paddan Aram, with his daughter Dinah. All the souls of his sons and his daughters were thirty-three. 16 The sons of Gad: Ziphion, Haggi, Shuni, Ezbon, Eri, Arodi, and Areli. 17 The sons of Asher: Imnah, Ishvah, Ishvi, Beriah, and Serah their sister. The sons of Beriah: Heber and Malchiel. 18 These are the sons of Zilpah, whom Laban gave to Leah, his daughter, and these she bore to Jacob, even sixteen souls. 19 The sons of Rachel, Jacob's wife: Joseph and Benjamin. 20 To Joseph in the land of Egypt were born Manasseh and Ephraim, whom Asenath, the daughter of Potiphera, priest of On, bore to him. 21 The sons of Benjamin: Bela, Becher, Ashbel, Gera, Naaman, Ehi, Rosh, Muppim, Huppim, and Ard. 22 These are the sons of Rachel, who were born to Jacob: all the souls were fourteen. 23 The son of Dan: Hushim. 24 The sons of Naphtali: Jahzeel, Guni, Jezer, and Shillem. 25 These are the sons of Bilhah, whom Laban gave to Rachel, his daughter, and these she bore to Jacob: all the souls were seven. 26 All the souls who came with Jacob into Egypt, who were his direct offspring, in addition to Jacob's sons' wives, all the souls were sixty-six. 27 The sons of Joseph, who were born to him in Egypt, were two souls. All the souls of the house of Jacob, who came into Egypt, were seventy.

Application

Verses 8-27 is a very long list of names pertaining to the genealogy of Jacob and his twelve sons down to several generations. The descendants of Jacob and his 12 sons in Egypt totaled 70 people. These initial 70 people would explode to more than 2 million at the time of Moses in 400 years' time! This was a fulfillment of the Abrahamic covenant, Genesis 15:13.

Genesis 15:13, *He said to Abram, "Know for sure that your offspring will live as foreigners in a land that is not theirs and will serve them. They will afflict them four hundred years."*

Verses 28-30, *28 Jacob sent Judah before him to Joseph, to show the way before him to Goshen, and they came into the land of Goshen. 29 Joseph prepared his chariot and went up to meet Israel, his father, in Goshen. He presented himself to him, and fell on his neck, and wept on his neck a good while. 30 Israel said to Joseph, "Now let me die since I have seen your face, that you are still alive."*

Application

Jacob and his company arrived at Goshen. Goshen is a fertile region of Egypt located to the east of the River Nile. Goshen in Hebrews means rain. Joseph presented himself to Jacob, fell on his neck, and wept uncontrollably. Jacob proclaimed that now that he had seen Joseph alive, he would be able to die in peace.

Verses 31-34, *31 Joseph said to his brothers, and to his father's house, "I will go up, and speak with Pharaoh, and will tell him, 'My brothers, and my father's house, who were in the land of Canaan, have come to me. 32 These men are shepherds, for they have been keepers of livestock, and they have brought their flocks, and their herds, and all that they have.' 33 It will happen when Pharaoh summons you and will say, 'What is your occupation?' 34 that you shall say, 'Your servants have been keepers of livestock from our youth even until now, both we, and our fathers:' that you may dwell in the land of Goshen; for every shepherd is an abomination to the Egyptians."*

Reflection

Joseph taught his brothers how to answer Pharoah when he asked them about their occupations. They were to reply that they were shepherds because shepherds were despised and ostracised by the Egyptians. By saying this, Pharoah would allow them to dwell in Goshen and the Egyptians would not try to intermingle with them.

God is a promise keeper. Abraham had Isaac and Isaac had son Jacob. Jacob had twelve sons and now seventy people entered Egypt. God keeps His promise and fulfills every one of them. Do not throw in the towel even when the going is tough. Hang in there, wait upon the LORD, with faith, perseverance, and obedience. When you looked back at your life story years later, you will realize that God is sovereign, and His providence is at work in your life.

Application

Genesis 46 tells the story of Jacob and his family traveling from Israel to Egypt, reuniting with Joseph, and eventually settling in Goshen. This chapter emphasizes themes such as God's guidance, family unity and faithfulness.

Trusting in God's Guidance

Jacob understood the value of trusting in the Lord even if His direction leads him into unfamiliar or challenging situations.

When making decisions, pray and seek guidance from God, trusting His leading even if it takes you out of your comfort zone.

Importance of Family Unity

Jacob's journey with his entire family from Canaan to Egypt illustrates the significance of family togetherness during times of change and transition.

Prioritize family unity and support during significant life transitions. Strengthen the bonds within your family unit by staying close and supporting one another.

God's faithfulness to His promises

God fulfilled His promise to make Jacob into a great nation in Egypt.

Take a moment to reflect on how God has faithfully kept his promises to you throughout your life. Trust in God's faithfulness, even when times are tough.

Cling to Him when times become uncertain.!

Obedience and Faith

Jacob's obedience to God in obeying Him by traveling to Egypt was an example of faith and trusting in IIis plan for his good.

Obeying God's promptings, even when they involve difficult choices, helps you learn obedience. Your trust in God's good plans for your benefit strengthens your faith.

Embracing New Beginnings

Jacob and his family welcomed God's plan for them when they relocated to Egypt as part of their greater future.

Be open to new opportunities and changes in your life, and believe that they can bring growth and blessings.

God's provision in difficult times

Jacob and his family found refuge in Egypt during an extended famine, showing God's provision in difficult times.

When going through difficult times, trust in His provision. He will meet all your needs and provide for you in ways you may never expect!

The joy of reconciliation

Jacob and Joseph's emotional reunion embodies the beauty and healing that come from reconciled relationships and renewed bonds.

Find ways to repair damaged relationships and work towards reconciliation. This will bring you joy as you mend broken bonds.

Acknowledging God's Sovereignty

God had arranged Jacob's journey to Egypt as part of His divine plan for their people, demonstrating His complete control over history.

Recognize and trust God's sovereignty over your life. Have faith that He has a plan, even when situations appear chaotic or uncertain.

Reflecting on Genesis 46 can inspire you to have faith in the Lord's guidance, prioritize family unity, embrace new beginnings, and trust in His faithfulness and provision in every aspect of your lives.

Prayer

Heavenly Father, thank You that You are a promise keeper. We claim all Your promises in the Bible and believe that they will come to pass. We claim the promises that Jesus Christ will come back again in the future to take us back to Him. Help us to see the bigger picture and not major in the minor, in Jesus' name, Amen.

Genesis 47

Sojourn in Egypt

Genesis 47 reveals Joseph's interactions with Pharaoh, as well as his leadership of Egypt during its famine period.

Verses 1-4, *1 Then Joseph went in and told Pharaoh, and said, "My father and my brothers, with their flocks, their herds, and all that they own, have come out of the land of Canaan; and behold, they are in the land of Goshen." 2 From among his brothers he took five men and presented them to Pharaoh. 3 Pharaoh said to his brothers, "What is your occupation?" They said to Pharaoh, "Your servants are shepherds, both we, and our fathers." 4 They also said to Pharaoh, "We have come to live as foreigners in the land, for there is no pasture for your servants' flocks. For the famine is severe in the land of Canaan. Now, therefore, please let your servants, dwell in the land of Goshen."*

Reflection

Joseph reported to Pharoah that his father and family had arrived in Goshen. He presented five of his brothers to Pharoah. When Pharaoh asked them about their occupation, they replied that they and their ancestors were shepherds of the flock. They explained that they were here as foreigners because they could not survive the famine in Canaan.

Verses 5-10, *5 Pharaoh spoke to Joseph, saying, "Your father and your brothers have come to you. 6 The land of Egypt is before you. Make your father and your brothers dwell in the best of the land. Let them dwell in the land of Goshen. If you know any able men among them, then put them in charge of my livestock." 7 Joseph brought in Jacob, his father, and set him before Pharaoh; and Jacob blessed Pharaoh. 8 Pharaoh said to Jacob, "How old are you?" 9 Jacob said to Pharaoh, "The years of my pilgrimage are one hundred thirty years. The days of the years of my life have been few and evil. They have not attained to the days of the years of the life of my fathers in the days of their pilgrimage." 10 Jacob blessed Pharaoh and went out from the presence of Pharaoh.*

Reflection

Pharoah extended his hospitality to Joseph's family and gave his blessing for them to stay in Goshen. He even invited Joseph's family members to work as shepherds for the Egyptians. Joseph presented Jacob to Pharoah. When Pharoah asked Jacob how old he was, he humbly replied that he was 130 years old. He told Pharoah that his life was nothing to brag about and his achievements fell short of his ancestor's expectations. Jacob blessed Pharoah and left the palace.

Verses 11-13, *11 Joseph placed his father and his brothers, and gave them a possession in the land of Egypt, in the best of the land, in the land of Rameses, as Pharaoh had commanded. 12 Joseph provided his father, his brothers, and all of his father's household with bread, according to the sizes of their families. 13 There was no bread in all the land; for the famine was very severe, so that the land of Egypt and the land of Canaan fainted by reason of the famine.*

Reflection

Joseph settled his family in the land of Rameses, another name for Goshen. Even though the famine was severe in the land, Joseph provided sufficient bread for every household, according to their family size.

Verses 14-16, *14 Joseph gathered up all the money that was found in the land of Egypt, and in the land of Canaan, for the grain which they bought: and Joseph brought the money into Pharaoh's house. 15 When the money was all spent in the land of Egypt, and in the land of Canaan, all the Egyptians came to Joseph, and said, "Give us bread, for why should we die in your presence? For our money fails." 16 Joseph said, "Give me your livestock, and I will give you food for your livestock if your money is gone."*

Reflection

Joseph brought all the proceeds from the sale of grains to Pharoah. Very soon, the people had no more money to buy grains. Their money had failed! Joseph allowed the people to barter trade using their livestock in exchange for bread.

Verses 17-19, *17 They brought their livestock to Joseph, and Joseph gave them bread in exchange for the horses, and for the flocks, and for the herds, and for the donkeys: and he fed them with bread in exchange for all their livestock for that year. 18 When that year was ended, they came to him the second year, and said to him, "We will not hide from my lord how our money is all spent, and the herds of livestock are my lord's. There is nothing left in the sight of my lord, but our bodies, and our lands. 19 Why should we die before your eyes, both we and our land? Buy us and our land for bread, and we and our land will be servants to Pharaoh. Give us seed, that we may live, and not die, and that the land won't be desolate."*

Reflection

By the end of the year, the people ran out of livestock and could not buy any more bread. They sold themselves into slavery and gave up their land to Pharoah in exchange for bread to stay alive.

Verses 20-24, *20 So, Joseph bought all the land of Egypt for Pharaoh, for every man of the Egyptians sold his field, because the famine was severe on them, and the land became Pharaoh's. 21 As for the people, he moved them to the cities from one end of the border of Egypt even to the other end of it. 22 Only he didn't buy the land of the priests, for the priests had a portion from Pharaoh, and ate their portion which Pharaoh gave them. That is why they didn't sell their land. 23 Then Joseph said to the people, "Behold, I have bought you and your land today for Pharaoh. Behold, here is seed for you, and you shall sow the land. 24 It will happen at the harvests, that you shall give a fifth to Pharaoh, and four parts will be your own, for seed of the field, for your food, for them of your households, and for food for your little ones."*

Reflection

Joseph bought all the land for Pharoah, except the land of the priest because the priests had a special allocation of bread by the palace. Joseph was very smart. He commanded the people would work on their land and give back one-fifth of the harvest to Pharoah as taxation. This worked out to be a win-win situation for everyone.

Verses 26-28, *25 They said, "You have saved our lives! Let us find favor in the sight of my lord, and we will be Pharaoh's servants." 26 Joseph made it a statute concerning the land of Egypt to this day, that Pharaoh should have the fifth. Only the land of the priests alone didn't become Pharaoh's.*

Reflection

The people acknowledged Joseph to be their savior. Without Joseph, they would have died of starvation.

Verses 27-31, *27 Israel lived in the land of Egypt, in the land of Goshen; and they got themselves possessions therein, and were fruitful, and multiplied exceedingly. 28 Jacob lived in the land of Egypt seventeen years. So the days of Jacob, the years of his life, were one hundred forty-seven years. 29 The time came near that Israel must die, and he called his son Joseph, and said to him, "If now*

I have found favor in your sight, please put your hand under my thigh, and deal kindly and truly with me. Please don't bury me in Egypt, 30 but when I sleep with my fathers, you shall carry me out of Egypt, and bury me in their burying place." Joseph said, "I will do as you have said." 31 Israel said, "Swear to me," and he swore to him. Then Israel bowed himself on the bed's head.

Reflection

By now, the famine was over. Jacob and his family successfully planted crops, prospered, and multiplied exceedingly. Jacob lived in Goshen for seventeen years and was one hundred and forty-seven years old. As Jacob was dying, he summoned Joseph to swear not to bury him in Egypt but to bury him in the cave of Machpelah where Abraham, Isaac, Sarah, and Leah were buried, Genesis 23: 17-18. Joseph put his hand under Jacob's thigh and swore to Jacob. Swearing with a hand under the thigh was an ancient custom, see Genesis 24:2.

Genesis 23:17-18, *"So, the field of Ephron, which was in Machpelah, which was before Mamre, the field, the cave which was in it, and all the trees that were in the field, that were in all of its borders, were deeded to Abraham for a possession in the presence of the children of Heth, before all who went in at the gate of his city."*

Genesis 24:2, *Abraham said to his servant, the elder of his house, who ruled over all that he had, "Please put your hand under my thigh."*

Jacob considered his stay in Egypt only as a pilgrim. As Christians, we are only pilgrims here on earth. This world is not our home, and we are just passing through. Do not hold on so tightly to the things here on earth. Our real home is in Heaven. When we leave this world at the end of our lives, we will be in Heaven with The Lord.

Joseph was very honest. He gave all the proceeds from the sale of grains to Pharaoh. Honesty is the best policy. God will reward your honesty and integrity.

Money and possession will fail you when recessions hit hard. Your only assurance is in God. God will never fail you. He will never leave you nor forsake you in your times of trouble. He will be with you through the storms of life.

Joseph is a type of Christ. He saved the lives of all the people of Egypt and the then-known world. Without Joseph, the people would die from starvation. Jesus is our Lord and Saviour. Without Christ, we will die in our sins.

Application

Here are a few key takeaways from this chapter.

Wise stewardship

Joseph's resourceful management during the famine showcases the importance of wise stewardship.

To make the best use of your resources, plan and budget carefully. Use the available resources wisely and anticipate future needs.

Caring for family

Joseph secured prime land in Goshen to sustain his family during the famine.

Take care in meeting the needs of your family. Prioritize their wellbeing and support them during times of troubled waters to make sure they have everything necessary for flourishing.

Trust in God's provision

Jacob and his family experienced God's provision through Joseph's position in Egypt, which enabled them to survive during a severe famine.

Believe that He will take care of your family's needs. Trust Him with this, and be grateful for His presence during difficult times!

Adaptability and flexibility

Egyptians had to adjust to new economic realities by resorting to barter trading for food when their money failed! Some even had to sell themselves to slavery.

Some people trust in horses and chariots, but it is better to trust in God. Eventually your money will fail you! Be prepared to modify plans and strategies to adjust to new threats and overcome unexpected obstacles that arise.

Integrity in Leadership

Joseph demonstrated unwavering integrity and fairness while effectively managing severe famine conditions.

Exercise integrity in decision-making, working to be fair and just. Seek to ensure that your actions benefit others as well as reflect your values.

Gratitude and appreciation

Joseph was acknowledged by the Egyptians for saving their lives during a famine with food supplies.

Practice gratitude every day by acknowledging and thanking those who help and support you and recognizing their contributions.

Honouring commitments

Joseph fulfilled his promise to his family by ensuring their settlement in Goshen and its prosperity.

Honor your commitments to others by being reliable and trustworthy while fulfilling promises and obligations made to others.

Long-Term Planning

Joseph's foresight and planning during Egypt's years of plenty enabled it to remain ready during times of famine.

Plan ahead, save resources, and make decisions that will help you in the future.

Role of government and social responsibility

Joseph's leadership demonstrated how important government leaders can be to ensuring societal well-being.

Advocate for ethical leadership in your community and government. Support policies that promote the common good and help those in need.

Genesis 47 can help you learn about managing resources wisely, taking care of family, trusting in God's provision, and practicing honesty and thankfulness in work and personal life.

Prayer

Heavenly Father, thank You for salvation, justification, the forgiveness of sins, and the gift of eternal life. Thank You for all that You have done in our lives. We confessed that we are sinners saved by grace. Help us to lead lives worthy of our calling, in Jesus' name, Amen.

Genesis 48

Inter-generational blessings

At the end of his life, Jacob adopted the two sons of Ephraim and Manasseh. Joseph would replace Rueben his firstborn son. Because the firstborn was entitled to a double share of the inheritance, Joseph would inherit two tribes, via Ephraim and Manasseh. Ephraim and Manasseh were also called the half tribes of Israel.

Verse 1-4, *1 After these things, someone said to Joseph, "Behold, your father is sick." He took with him his two sons, Manasseh and Ephraim. 2 Someone told Jacob, and said, "Behold, your son Joseph comes to you," and Israel strengthened himself, and sat on the bed. 3 Jacob said to Joseph, "God Almighty appeared to me at Luz in the land of Canaan, and blessed me, 4 and said to me, 'Behold, I will make you fruitful, and multiply you, and I will make of you a company of peoples, and will give this land to your offspring after you for an everlasting possession.'*

Reflection

As mentioned before, 'after these things' is a time marker between Genesis 11 and 12, but the length of time could not be ascertained. Joseph brought his sons Manasseh and Ephraim to Jacob for blessing. Jacob or Israel gathered all his strength and sat on his bed. He told Joseph that Almighty God, El Shaddai, appeared to him at Bethel. The LORD blessed him and gave him an everlasting covenant of posterity and land, Genesis 28:13-14.

Genesis 28:13-13, *"There above it stood the Lord, and he said: "I am the Lord, the God of your father Abraham and the God of Isaac. I will give you and your descendants the land on which you are lying. Your descendants will be like the dust of the earth, and you will spread out to the west and to the east, to the north and to the south. All peoples on earth will be blessed through you and your offspring."*

Verses 5-7, *5 Now your two sons, who were born to you in the land of Egypt before I came to you into Egypt, are mine; Ephraim and Manasseh, even as Reuben and Simeon, will be mine. 6 Your offspring, whom you become the father of after them, will be yours. They will be called after the name of their brothers in their inheritance. 7 As for me, when I came from Paddan, Rachel died beside me in the land of Canaan on the way, when there was still some distance to come to Ephrath, and I buried her there on the way to Ephrath (also called Bethlehem)."*

Reflection

Jacob told Joseph that he would adopt his sons Ephraim and Manasseh to be his first and second sons superseding Rueben and Simeon for inheritance purposes. Jacob told Joseph about the death and burial of Joseph's mother Rachel, in Bethlehem, Genesis 35:16-18.

Genesis 35:16-18, *They traveled from Bethel. There was still some distance to come to Ephrath, and Rachel travailed. She had hard labor. 17 When she was in hard labor, the midwife said to her, "Don't be afraid, for now, you will have another son." As her soul was departing (for she died), she named him Benoni, but his father named him Benjamin.*

Verses 8-11, *8 Israel saw Joseph's sons, and said, "Who are these?" 9 Joseph said to his father, "They are my sons, whom God has given me here." He said, "Please bring them to me, and I will bless them." 10 Now the eyes of Israel were dim for age so that he couldn't see well. Joseph brought them near to him, and he kissed them and embraced them. 11 Israel said to Joseph, "I didn't think I would see your face, and behold, God has let me see your offspring also."*

Reflection

Jacob's vision was poor, and he could not see clearly. Joseph brought his sons near to Jacob and Jacob kissed and embraced them. Jacob thanked God for allowing him to see Joseph and his sons before his death.

Verses 12-14, *12 Joseph brought them out from between his knees, and he bowed himself with his face to the earth. 13 Joseph took them both, Ephraim in his right hand toward Israel's left hand, and Manasseh in his left hand toward Israel's right hand, and brought them near to him. 14 Israel stretched out his right hand and laid it on Ephraim's head, who was the younger, and his left hand on Manasseh's head, guiding his hands knowingly, for Manasseh was the firstborn.*

Reflection

Joseph placed Manasseh on his left and Ephraim on his right facing Jacob for a blessing. To Joseph's surprise, Jacob crossed his hand in the form of a cross, placing his right hand on Ephraim's head and his left hand on Manasseh's head.

Verses 15-16, *15 He blessed Joseph, and said, "The God before whom my fathers, Abraham and Isaac walked, the God who has fed me all my life long to this day, 16 the angel who has redeemed me from all evil, bless the lads and let my name be named on them, and the name of my fathers, Abraham and Isaac. Let them grow into a multitude upon the earth."*

Reflection

Jacob pronounced a blessing on Joseph, calling upon the LORD as the God of Abraham and Isaac to give him posterity.

Verses 17–20, *17 When Joseph saw that his father laid his right hand on the head of Ephraim, it displeased him. He held up his father's hand, to remove it from Ephraim's head to Manasseh's head. 18 Joseph said to his father, "Not so, my father, for this is the firstborn. Put your right hand on his head." 19 His father refused, and said, "I know, my son, I know. He also will become a people, and he also will be great. However, his younger brother will be greater than he, and his offspring will become a multitude of nations." 20 He blessed them that day, saying, "Israel will bless in you, saying, 'God make you as Ephraim and as Manasseh'" He set Ephraim before Manasseh.*

Reflection

Joseph tried to remove Jacob's hands so that his right hand would be over Manasseh's head and his left hand over Ephraim's head, but Jacob refused, saying that his blessing was for Ephraim first and for Manasseh second.

Verses 21-22, *21 Israel said to Joseph, "Behold, I am dying, but God will be with you, and bring you again to the land of your fathers. 22 Moreover I have given to you one portion above your brothers, which I took out of the hand of the Amorite with my sword and with my bow."*

Reflection

Jacob assured Joseph that God would be with him and would bring him back to Canaan. Jacob gave Joseph a double portion of the inheritance.

Exodus 13:9, Joseph died in Egypt but 400 years later, Moses brought his bones back to Canaan.

Exodus 13:19, *Moses took the bones of Joseph with him, for he had made the children of Israel swear, saying, "God will surely visit you, and you shall carry up my bones away from here with you."*

Jacob adopted his grandsons Ephraim and Manasseh to be his own sons. This is a picture of God adopting us into His family as His sons, Galatians 3:26, Romans 8:15, Romans 9:26.

Galatians 3:26, *"For you are all children of God, through faith in Christ Jesus."*

Romans 8:15, *For you didn't receive the spirit of bondage again to fear, but you received the Spirit of adoption, by whom we cry, "Abba! Father!"*

Romans 9:26, *"It will be that in the place where it was said to them, 'You are not my people,' there they will be called 'children of the living God.'"*

Ephraim the younger became the first and Manasseh the first born became second. This also happened to Isaac and Ishmael, Jacob, and Esau. In the Kingdom of God, the first can become last and the last can become first. Matthew 20:16.

Matthew 20:16, *"So, the last will be first, and the first last. For many are called, but few chosen."*

Application

Genesis 48 tells the story of Jacob adopting Joseph's sons Ephraim and Manasseh, and prophesying over them. Below are some applications gleaned from this chapter.

Recognizing Elders and Their Wisdom

Joseph brought his sons for blessings from their grandfather Jacob, showing respect for his wisdom and spiritual authority.

Respect and seek advice from older family members and mentors. Learn from their experiences and insights for your own benefit.

God Is in Charge of Selecting Leaders

Jacob favored Ephraim over Manasseh to show that God's choices don't always match human expectations.

Trust God and His plans for leadership and blessings in your life, even when they are different from what is traditionally expected or normal.

Blessings and Inheritance

Jacob's blessings on Ephraim and Manasseh emphasize the importance of passing down spiritual blessings and faith to future generations.

Faith in God's Promises

Jacob displayed unfaltering faith in the promises made to his descendants by God to become a great nation.

Stay faithful to your beliefs, even when things seem uncertain. Trust that God will fulfill His promises at the perfect time.

Overcoming Cultural Norms

Jacob defied cultural norms by selecting Ephraim as the younger son, emphasizing the superiority of God's ways over human traditions.

Passing Faith On

Jacob included a prayer for God to bless his sons as part of his blessing to demonstrate the importance of passing down personal relationships with God through generations.

Recognizing God's Hand in Your Life

Jacob acknowledged God as his shepherd and gave thanks for His guidance and care throughout his journey.

Take some time today to reflect upon and acknowledge God's hand in your life. Express thanks for the way He guides and supports your journey!

Intergenerational Blessings

Jacob extended his blessings beyond just his sons to include his grandchildren, underscoring the importance of intergenerational blessings.

Think about how you can help future generations. Pray and invest in their spiritual growth and well-being. This includes your grandchildren and generations after them.

Genesis 48 can help you see God's blessings, respect the wisdom of your elders, and act in faith for future generations.

Prayer

Heavenly Father, thank You for giving us the spirit of adoption so that we can call You Abba Father. Thank You that in the Kingdom of God, we have spiritual brothers and sisters in Christ to care for each other in times of need, in Jesus' name, Amen.

Genesis 49

Death of Jacob

Jacob came to the end of his life at the ripe old age of 147 years. On his deathbed, Jacob gathered his sons around him, to bless, censure, and prophesy over the future of their tribes.

Verses 1-4, *1 Jacob called to his sons and said: "Gather yourselves together, that I may tell you that which will happen to you in the days to come. 2 Assemble yourselves, and hear, you sons of Jacob. Listen to Israel, your father. 3 "Reuben, you are my firstborn, my might, and the beginning of my strength, excelling in dignity and excelling in power. 4 Boiling over like water, you shall not excel, because you went up to your father's bed, then defiled it. He went up to my couch.*

Reflection

Jacob summoned all his sons to hear what he would say for the very last time. He started with his eldest son Reuben. As the firstborn son, he should inherit the birthright and a double portion of the inheritance but this did not happen. Jacob gave the birthright to Joseph and his sons Ephraim and Manasseh each received a tribe. Reuben forfeited his birthright because he committed incest with his stepmother Bilhah forty years ago.

Verses 5-7, *5 Simeon and Levi are brothers. Their swords are weapons of violence. 6 My soul, don't come into their council. My glory, don't be united to their assembly; for in their anger, they killed men. In their self-will they hamstrung cattle. 7 Cursed be their anger, for it was fierce; and their wrath, for it was cruel. I will divide them in Jacob, and scatter them in Israel.*

Reflection

Simeon and Levi were censured for their cruelty when they murdered all the males in Shechem over the incident of their sister Dinah's rape, Genesis 34:25-26. The tribe of Levi did not get any allotment of land and the tribe of Simeon was not a significant tribe.

Genesis 34:25-26 *"Three days later, when they were sore, two of Jacob's sons, Simeon and Levi, the brothers of Dinah, each took his sword, came upon the unsuspecting city, and killed all he males. They killed Hamor and Shechem, his son, and took Dinah out of Shechem's house and went away."*

Verses 8-12, *8 Judah, your brothers will praise you. Your hand will be on the neck of your enemies. Your father's sons will bow down before you. 9 Judah is a lion's cub. From the prey, my son, you have gone up. He stooped down, he crouched as a lion, as a lioness. Who will rouse him up? 10 The scepter will not depart from Judah, nor the ruler's staff from between his feet, until he comes to whom it belongs. The obedience of the people will be to him. 11 Binding his foal to the vine, his donkey's colt to the choice vine, he has washed his garments in wine, his robes in the blood of grapes. 12 His eyes will be red with wine, his teeth white with milk.*

Reflection

Judah started off badly. He suggested to his brothers to sell Joseph to get monetary gain out of it. He married a Canaanite woman and committed incest with his daughter-in-law Tamar.

However, he ended well. He placed his neck on the chopping board and stood as collateral for the safe return of Benjamin to Jacob. The scepter will not depart from Judah. The scepter is a royal staff belonging to a king. King David and Jesus Christ were descendants from the tribe of Judah. Jesus Christ is the Lion of Judah.

Verses 13-21, *13 Zebulun will dwell at the haven of the sea. He will be for a haven of ships. His border will be on Sidon. 14 "Issachar is a strong donkey, lying down between the saddlebags. 15 He saw a resting place, that it was good, the land, that it was pleasant. He bows his shoulder to the burden and becomes a servant doing forced labor. 16 Dan will judge his people, as one of the tribes of Israel. 17 Dan will be a serpent on the trail, an adder in the path, that bites the horse's heels so that his rider falls backward. 18 I have waited for your salvation, Yahweh. 19 A troop will press on Gad, but he will press on their heel. 20 Asher's food will be rich. He will produce royal dainties. 21 Napthali is a doe set free, who bears beautiful fawns.*

Reflection

The descendants of Zebulun were sea dwellers. The descendants of Issachar were archers and skilful with bows and arrows. The descendants of Dan were like serpents. The descendants of Asher would be rich. The descendants of Naphtali were beautiful as does.

Verses 22-27, *22 "Joseph is a fruitful vine, a fruitful vine by a spring. His branches run over the wall. 23 The archers have severely grieved him, shot at him, and persecuted him: 24 But his bow remained strong. The arms of his hands were made strong, by the hands of the Mighty One of Jacob, (from there is the shepherd, the stone of Israel), 25 even by the God of your father, who will help you, by the Almighty, who will bless you, with blessings of heaven above, blessings of the deep that lies below, blessings of the breasts, and of the womb. 26 The blessings of your father have prevailed above the blessings of your ancestors, above the boundaries of the ancient hills. They will be on the head of Joseph, on the crown of the head of him who is separated from his brothers. 27 "Benjamin is a ravenous wolf. In the morning, he will devour the prey. At evening he will divide the plunder."*

Reflection

Joseph was a fruitful vine. At the tender age of seventeen years, he suffered at the hands of his brothers and sold as a slave to Egypt. He was falsely accused of rape and languished in prison for years. However, he was strong, faithful, and obedient to the LORD.

After interpreting Pharoah's dreams, he was released and promoted to become the Prime Minister of Egypt. Jacob called the LORD, the mighty One of Jacob, the shepherd, the stone of Israel, the God of Joseph's father, the Almighty (El Shaddai). Jacob pronounced the LORD's blessings upon Joseph. The descendants of Benjamin were like ravenous wolves, ready to devour and plunder their preys in the morning and evening.

Verses 28-33, *28 All these are the twelve tribes of Israel, and this is what their father spoke to them, and blessed them. He blessed everyone according to his own blessing. 29 He instructed them, and said to them, "I am to be gathered to my people. Bury me with my fathers in the cave that is in the field of Ephron the Hittite, 30 in the cave that is in the field of Machpelah, which is before Mamre, in the land of Canaan, which Abraham bought with the field from Ephron the Hittite as a burial place. 31 There they buried Abraham and Sarah, his wife. There they buried Isaac and Rebekah, his wife, and there I buried Leah: 32 the field and the cave that is therein, which was purchased from the children of Heth." 33 When Jacob finished charging his sons, he gathered up his feet into the bed, breathed his last breath, and was gathered to his people.*

Reflection

After pronouncing his blessings and prophecies, Jacob commanded his sons to bury him in Canaan in the cave of Machpelah. This was the land Abraham purchased from Ephron, the Hittite as a burial plot for his wife Sarah, Genesis

23:17-18. Isaac, Rebekah, and Leah were also buried here. After this, Jacob gave up his spirit and died.

Genesis 23:17-18, *"So, the field of Ephron, which was in Machpelah, which was before Mamre, the field, the cave which was in it, and all the trees that were in the field, that were in all of its borders, were deeded to Abraham for a possession in the presence of the children of Heth, before all who went in at the gate of his city."*

Jesus Christ is the Lion from the tribe of Judah. He is the Savior of the world, the second person of the Trinitarian God of the Bible. Whoever believed in Him shall not perish but have everlasting life, John 3:16.

John 3:16, *"For God so loved the world, that he gave his one and only Son, that whoever believes in him should not perish, but have eternal life."*

Application

Genesis 49 tells about Jacob's last words and blessings for each of his twelve sons, who represent the twelve tribes of Israel, during their inheritance ceremony. Jacob provided insight into their future while reflecting different aspects of their character and destiny through these blessings. Here are some applications from Genesis 49:

Understanding the impact of your action

Jacob's blessings and prophecies for his sons were influenced by both their past actions - both good and bad. He gave them advice that would protect them in difficult times and praised their accomplishments.

Consider how the actions you take now could have an effect on both yourself and others in the future. Strive to live with integrity and make decisions that positively influence your legacy.

The power of words

Jacob's words had an indelible mark on his sons' futures, exemplifying how words can either bless or curse.

Be conscious of your words' power. Use them for encouragement, upliftment, and blessing rather than hurting or insulting someone.

Recognizing and utilizing your strengths

Jacob highlighted the unique strengths and characteristics of each of his sons, while acknowledging their individual roles and contributions.

Recognize your individual talents, capabilities and characteristics, so you can use them positively within your community to fulfill your purpose.

Accountability and consequences

Some of Jacob's sons received negative prophecies as punishment for past wrongdoings, demonstrating the lasting ramifications of actions taken.

Acknowledging and taking responsibility for your actions will allow for lasting changes to take effect and correct misdeeds as needed.

Emphasizing the importance of leadership

Judah was blessed to become the ancestor of Jesus despite his shortcomings.

Recognize the significance of leadership and its characteristics. Aim to cultivate these traits within yourself while supporting ethical leadership within your community.

The significance of legacy

Jacob's blessings demonstrated the significance of family legacy.

Think about the impact you have on others. Strive to leave a lasting positive impression on your loved ones and the community.

Hope and Redemption

Despite their past errors, some of Jacob's sons received uplifting and redeeming blessings, illustrating the potential for change and redemption.

Honoring Family Heritage

Jacob was careful to honor both his family legacy and God's promises for his descendants when making his last remarks.

Acknowledge and value the positive values that have been inherited from your family's legacy. Use these values as a foundation to pursue and fulfill God's plans in your life.

Prophetic Insight and Planning

Jacob used God's prophetic insight to provide direction for his family's future. To follow Jacob's example, seek spiritual guidance and prophetic insight for yourself to plan your future with prayerful discernment, trusting that He has His hand on your path.

Dealing with conflict and forgiveness

Jacob's blessings shed light on his complicated relationships and family divisions, while conveying a message of healing and unity.

Approach family or community conflicts with a mindset of reconciliation and forgiveness, aiming for unity and peace despite differences.

Genesis 49 can help you realize the significance of your actions, words, and the impact they have. Reflection also enables you to seek God's guidance while building positive legacies, while cultivating unity and hope among your relationships.

Prayer

Heavenly Father, thank You for sending Your Son Jesus Christ into the world to be the atoning sacrifice for our sins. Thank You for salvation, the forgiveness of sins, justification, and eternal life. Thank You that we can call upon Your name in prayer any time with boldness and confidence, in Jesus' name, Amen.

Genesis 50
Death of Joseph

The <u>Book of</u> Genesis ended with the death of Joseph. After Jacob's death, Joseph embalmed his body and brought his remains back to Canaan, and buried him in the cave of Machpelah in Hebron. As the narrative continued, Joseph reached the end of his life at a ripe old age of 110 years. Joseph made his brothers swear on his deathbed that their descendants would carry his bones back to Canaan. Joseph was buried in Egypt but 400 years later, Moses carried Joseph's bones back to Canaan, Exodus 13:19.

Exodus 13:19, *Moses took the bones of Joseph with him, for he had made the children of Israel swear, saying, "God will surely visit you, and you shall carry up my bones away from here with you."*

Verses 1-5, *1 Joseph fell on his father's face, wept on him, and kissed him. 2 Joseph commanded his servants, the physicians, to embalm his father; and the physicians embalmed Israel. 3 Forty days were used for him, for that is how many the days it takes to embalm. The Egyptians wept for Israel for seventy days. 4 When the days of weeping for him were past, Joseph spoke to Pharaoh's staff, saying, "If now I have found favor in your eyes, please speak in the ears of Pharaoh, saying, 5 'My father made me swear, saying, "Behold, I am dying. Bury me in my grave which I have dug for myself in the land of Canaan." Now, therefore, please let me go up and bury my father, and I will come again.'"*

Reflection

After Jacob's death, Joseph instructed the physicians to embalm his body for over forty days. The Egyptians mourned for Jacob for seventy days. After this, Joseph sought permission from Pharoah to send Jacob's remains back to Canaan.

Verses 6-10, *6 Pharaoh said, "Go up, and bury your father, just like he made you swear." 7 Joseph went up to bury his father; and with him went up all the servants of Pharaoh, the elders of his house, all the elders of the land of Egypt, 8 all the house of Joseph, his brothers, and his father's house. Only their little ones, their flocks, and their herds, they left in the land of Goshen. 9 Both chariots and horsemen went up with him. It was a very great company. 10 They came to the threshing floor of Atad, which is beyond the Jordan, and there they lamented with a very great and severe lamentation. He mourned for his father seven days.*

Reflection

Pharoah was very supportive and willingly agreed to Joseph's request. Joseph, his brothers and their families brought Jacob's remains back to Canaan accompanied by Egyptian chariots and horsemen. They reached the threshing floor of Atad beyond the Jordan and mourned for seven days.

Verses 11-14, *11 When the inhabitants of the land, the Canaanites, saw the mourning in the floor of Atad, they said, "This is a grievous mourning by the Egyptians." Therefore, its name was called Abel Mizraim, which is beyond the Jordan. 12 His sons did to him just as he commanded them, 13 for his sons carried him into the land of Canaan, and buried him in the cave of the field of Machpelah, which Abraham bought with the field, as a possession for a burial site, from Ephron the Hittite, near Mamre. 14 Joseph returned into Egypt—he, and his brothers, and all that went up with him to bury his father, after he had buried his father.*

Reflection

The Canaanites saw them mourning on the threshing floor of Atad. Atad was renamed Abel Mizraim, which in Hebrews, means the mourning of Egypt. Jacob's sons carried their father's remains and buried him in the cave of Machpelah. After this, the whole company returned to Egypt.

Verses 15-20, *15 When Joseph's brothers saw that their father was dead, they said, "It may be that Joseph will hate us, and will fully pay us back for all the evil which we did to him." 16 They sent a message to Joseph, saying, "Your father commanded before he died, saying, 17 'You shall tell Joseph, "Now please forgive the disobedience of your brothers, and their sin, because they did evil to you."' Now, please forgive the disobedience of the servants of the God of your father." Joseph wept when they spoke to him. 18 His brothers also went and fell down before his face; and they said, "Behold, we are your servants." 19 Joseph said to them, "Don't be afraid, for am I in the place of God? 20 As for you, you meant evil against me, but God meant it for good, to save many people alive, as is happening today.*

Reflection

After Jacob's burial, Joseph's brothers were worried that Joseph might take revenge on them. They sent a message to Joseph seeking forgiveness from him. Joseph wept and replied that he would not take revenge because he was not

God. Even though they intended to do evil to him, God intended it for good and used this incident to save many people including them.

Verses 21-26, *21 Now, therefore, don't be afraid. I will provide for you and your little ones." He comforted them and spoke kindly to them. 22 Joseph lived in Egypt, he, and his father's house. Joseph lived one hundred ten years. 23 Joseph saw Ephraim's children to the third generation. The children also of Machir, the son of Manasseh, were born on Joseph's knees. 24 Joseph said to his brothers, "I am dying, but God will surely visit you, and bring you up out of this land to the land which he swore to Abraham, to Isaac, and to Jacob." 25 Joseph took an oath from the children of Israel, saying, "God will surely visit you, and you shall carry up my bones from here." 26 So, Joseph died, being one hundred ten years old, and they embalmed him, and he was put in a coffin in Egypt.*

Reflection

Joseph comforted his brothers and took care of them and their families. Joseph lived up to a ripe old age of 110 years. He saw his son's children up to the third generation. On his deathbed, he commanded his brothers and their families to bring his bones back to Canaan in the future. After Joseph's death, his brothers embalmed him and buried him in Egypt. 400 years after this, Moses took Joseph's bones back to Canaan, Exodus 13:19.

Exodus 13:19, *Moses took the bones of Joseph with him, for he had made the children of Israel swear, saying, "God will surely visit you, and you shall carry up my bones away from here with you."*

Joseph's story is a story of God's providence. Even though Joseph's brothers intended to harm him, God had a plan to save him and his family. If not for Joseph, his father, brothers, and family would not have survived the famine. God's prophesy of taking Jacob's family out of Canaan into Egypt for 400 years would not have been fulfilled. This is Romans 8:28 at work. You can claim the promise of Romans 8:28.

Romans 8:28, *"We know that all things work together for good for those who love God, for those who are called according to his purpose."*

Application

Genesis 50 ends the story of Joseph and his brothers with Jacob's death and Joseph forgiving them. It examines themes such as reconciliation, fulfillment of God's promises and legacy.

Honor the Past

Joseph and his brothers respected Jacob's final wishes by transporting him for burial in Canaan.

Honor your ancestors by respecting family traditions and memories, and preserving their legacy through your actions.

The power of forgiveness

After Jacob's death, Joseph's brothers feared retribution, but Joseph reassured them of his forgiveness, emphasizing that God had a greater purpose.

Embrace and practice forgiveness. Let go of grudges and seek to understand how God can work through even painful circumstances for a greater good.

Providence

Joseph understood that what his brothers intended as harm, God used for good and saved many lives.

Trust God with your life and put your trust in His plans. They are designed for your ultimate good!

Provide care to others

Joseph demonstrated caring for others after his father's death by providing for their well-being and protecting those close to him, especially his siblings and families.

For you, this means taking care of your own family members by offering support, resources, and care when they need it the most.

Facing mortality with faith

Jacob and Joseph both faced death with great faith in God's promises. Joseph made his brothers promise that they would take his remains out of Egypt when God fulfilled His promise and brought them into the Promised Land.

Embrace mortality with unwavering faith and boundless optimism. Rely on God's promises, living your life in ways that reflect your belief in His faithfulness and future plans.

Legacy of faith

Joseph's request that his bones be brought back to Israel demonstrated his belief in God's promises made to his ancestors. Joseph trusted that everything would eventually end up where it was supposed to, just as God had promised.

Teach your children and others how to trust in God's promises and live a faithful life to leave a legacy of faith for the future.

Dealing with anxiety and fear

Joseph's brothers experienced uncertainty after Jacob died, yet Joseph provided comfort with kindness and forgiveness.

Reassure and comfort those experiencing anxiety by offering comfort, support and confidence that God provides peace.

Living out reconciliation

Joseph's reconciliation with his brothers was an impressive example of God's mercy and forgiveness.

Make a deliberate effort to take proactive steps in order to reconcile relationships. Seek to rebuild broken connections and practice grace and forgiveness as much as possible.

Embracing God's timing

Joseph's life exemplifies the wisdom of patience as he witnessed how His promises came true over many years.

Trust in God's timing when making plans and practice patience. His plans always unfold according to his perfect schedule, even if waiting is necessary.

Stay faithful in all circumstances

Joseph was faithful to God throughout all the challenges in his life, showing unwavering trust in his plan.

Stay true to God at all times. Trust that He is always working out a good plan in your life and believe He has it in mind for your ultimate good!

In Genesis 50, you can learn to live a life marked by faith, forgiveness, and responsibility. This means respecting the past and having faith in God's control and future plans.

Prayer

Heavenly Father, thank You for walking with us through the life of Joseph verse by verse, paragraph by paragraph, and chapter-by-chapter. We claim the promises of 2 Timothy 3:16 that scripture is inspired by You andis profitable for teaching, reproof, correction, and training in righteousness. Thank You for this wonderful experience, adventure, and spiritual journey, in Jesus' name, Amen.

One Last Thing

Thank you for choosing to read my book. I hope that it has provided you with an enjoyable and thought-provoking experience. Please give me your feedback on the book by writing a review on the platform or book review website where you bought it. Thank you! Your review will help other readers and I understand the book better. Your honest review will help me improve as a writer and create even better content in the future. Once again, thank you for giving my book a chance, and I sincerely hope that you found it worth your time.

Dr. Andrew C S Koh

Don't miss out!

Visit the website below and you can sign up to receive emails whenever Dr Andrew C S Koh publishes a new book. There's no charge and no obligation.

https://books2read.com/r/B-A-FMXV-SEEDC

BOOKS 2 READ

Connecting independent readers to independent writers.

Did you love *The Story of Joseph: Genesis 37-50*? Then you should read *Faith Journey of Abraham: Genesis 12-25*[1] by Dr Andrew C S Koh!

Experience the life of Abraham like never before in Dr. Andrew C. S. Koh's Faith Journey of Abraham. This Expository Commentary, Daily Devotion, and Bible Study Guide focuses on Genesis 12–25. It explores Abraham's faith journey and how it can still impact us today. It is easy to read and not academic. This book will convict, deepen, transform, mature, enrich, teach, and bless the reader's life. Readers will encounter God and His Word as they read, re-read, study, explore, and meditate on this book. The Faith Journey of Abraham is the perfect gift for those who wish to study the Book of Genesis systematically. It is comparable to other popular religion books such as Max Lucado's God's Story Your Story and John Ortberg's Who Is This Man? Experience the transformative power of the faith of Abraham.

Read more at https://www.drandrewcskoh.com.

---

1. https://books2read.com/u/bOnvB9

2. https://books2read.com/u/bOnvB9

Also by Dr Andrew C S Koh

Daily Devotion
Manna of Life: Daily Devotion

Daily Devotions
Bread of Life Daily Devotions
Words of Eternal Life
Bread From Heaven: Daily Devotions
Light of the World Daily Devotions
Light of the World Daily Devotions
The Way, the Truth, and the Life

Genesis
Understanding Genesis 1-11: From Adam to Abraham
Faith Journey of Abraham: Genesis 12-25
Life Story of Jacob: Genesis 26-36
The Story of Joseph: Genesis 37-50

Gospels and Act
The Gospel According to Matthew
Daily Devotion Gospel of Mark
The Gospel According to Luke

Daily Devotion Gospel of John
Acts: Volume 1 and 2, From Jerusalem to Rome

Non Pauline and General Epistles
Hebrews: the Just Shall Live by Faith
1 John, 2 John, 3 John & Jude: a Verse by Verse Bible Study
General Epistles: 1 Peter, 2 Peter, James

Pauline Epistles
Romans: The Just Shall Live by Faith
1 Corinthians: The Greatest of These is Love
2 Corinthians: My Grace is Sufficient for You
1 Thessalonians, 2 Thessalonians, Philemon
Pastoral Epistles: 1 Timothy, 2 Timothy, Titus
Galatians: Justified by Faith in Jesus Christ
Philemon: Charge to the Master's Account

Prison Epistles
The Prison Epistles
Philippians: Rejoice Always in the Lord
Colossians: He is the Image of the Invisible God
Ephesians: Every Spiritual Blessing in the Heavenly Places in Christ

Standalone
Apocalypse: Understanding the Book of Revelation
Expository Preaching
Memoirs of a Doctor
Moses: Let My People Go
The ABCS of Self-Publishing

Living Word Living Savior: a Portrait of Jesus Through the Eyes of John

Watch for more at https://www.drandrewcskoh.com.

About the Author

Dr. Andrew C. S. Koh is a Christian author who has published 36 books. Beyond his role as an author, he is also a blogger, podcaster, bible teacher, digital creator, and retired cardiologist. He pursued theology at Laidlaw College in Auckland, New Zealand in 1999. Currently residing in Malaysia with his family, he finds joy in coffee, travel, and photography. He is listed in the Malaysia Book of Records for having the Most Books Published and Released in 2021.

Find out more about Andrew on:

https://linktr.ee/andrewcskoh

Search Andrew's books on:

https://books2read.com/ap/xX066D/Dr-Andrew-C-S-Koh

Get your free books on:

https://storyoriginapp.com/giveaways/b295be58-7736-11ec-ac4b-e34d930c508e

https://books2read.com/u/3kYJlN

Read more at https://www.drandrewcskoh.com.

About the Publisher

Dr. Andrew C. S. Koh, a bestselling Amazon author, has authored 36 Christian books covering the New Testament, Old Testament, Bible study guides, and devotionals. Beyond his role as an author, he is a blogger, podcaster, bible teacher, and cardiologist. He pursued theology at Laidlaw College in Auckland, New Zealand in 1999.. Currently residing in Malaysia with his family, he finds joy in coffee, travel, and photography. He is listed in the Malaysia Book of Records for having the Most Books Published and Released in 2021.

Author of Memoirs of a Doctor:

https://dl.bookfunnel.com/hm2npovxom

Link Tree:

https://linktr.ee/andrewcskoh

Universal book link:

https://books2read.com/ap/xX066D/Dr-Andrew-C-S-Koh

New Release Notification:

https://books2read.com/author/dr-andrew-c-s-koh/subscribe/1/384961/

Free Books:

https://storyoriginapp.com/giveaways/b295be58-7736-11ec-ac4b-e34d930c508e

https://books2read.com/u/3kYJlN

Read more at https://www.drandrewcskoh.com.

www.ingramcontent.com/pod-product-compliance
Lightning Source LLC
Chambersburg PA
CBHW061328120726
48001CB00002B/738